D1111870

WALKING TOURS OF BOSTON'S MADE LAND

WALKING TOURS OF BOSTON'S MADE LAND

NANCY S. SEASHOLES

The MIT Press
Cambridge, Massachusetts
London, England

MIT Press books may be purchased at special quantity discounts for business or sales promotional use. For information, email special_sales@mitpress.mit.edu or write to Special Sales Department, The MIT Press, 55 Hayward Street, Cambridge, MA 02142.

This book was set in Garamond Three by The MIT Press.

Printed and bound in the United States of America.

Library of Congress Cataloging-in-Publication Data

Seasholes, Nancy S.
Walking tours of Boston's made land / Nancy S. Seasholes.
    p. cm.
Includes bibliographical references and index.
ISBN-13: 978-0-262-69339-4 (pbk. : alk. paper)
ISBN-10: 0-262-69339-9 (pbk. : alk. paper)
1. Boston (Mass.)—Tours. 2. Fills (Earthwork)—Massachusetts—Boston—Guidebooks.
3. Walking—Massachusetts—Boston—Guidebooks. I. Title.
F73.18.S43 2006
917.44'610444—dc22
                                                                    2006019360

10 9 8 7 6 5 4 3 2 1

CONTENTS

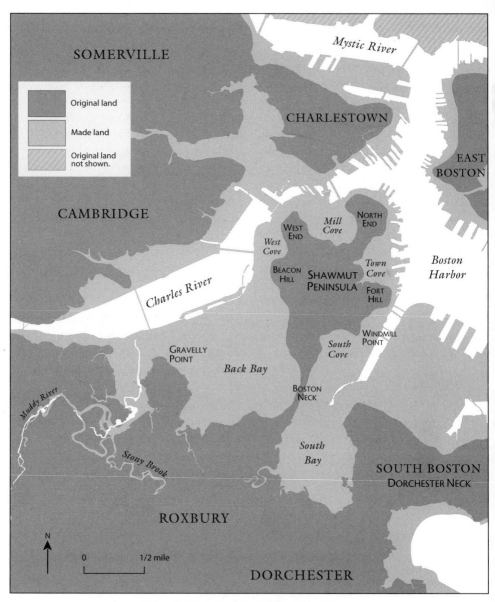

Map of Original and Made Land in Boston

PREFACE

Imagine yourself in front of Boston's Faneuil Hall, that venerable Revolutionary War–era landmark. On the land between you and the waterfront would be the Sam Adams statue, Faneuil Hall itself, Quincy Market, Marketplace Center, and Christopher Columbus Park. But what if you were in the same spot in 1630, the year Boston was founded? You would be standing in water (or perhaps mud, at low tide) at the head of a large cove, and the sites of those buildings and park would be water, too. Where did the present land come from? It was *made* by filling in tidal flats—areas covered with water at high tide and exposed mud flats at low—a process I call *landmaking*.

The area between Faneuil Hall and the waterfront is not the only part of Boston where landmaking has occurred. In fact, looking at the map opposite, which shows the original and present land areas of Boston, you can see that many parts of the city have large areas of made land. Actually, about one-sixth of Boston is on fill, though because this figure includes many inland areas with no made land at all, the proportion is much higher in sections along the harbor or rivers. The original Boston peninsula and Charlestown have both been doubled by landmaking, for example.

This transformation of Boston's topography by landmaking is an important part of the city's history. Understanding where land was made can help us understand many aspects of present Boston. If you've ever wondered why street grids in adjacent areas don't mesh, for example, it's often because those areas were filled at different times. Or, if you've noticed that architectural styles in Back Bay progress from those popular in the 1860s, near Arlington Street, to those in vogue in the 1880s, near Massachusetts Avenue, it is because Back Bay was filled from east to west over a period of thirty years. And of course knowing where and how landmaking occurred is essential for dealing with problems created by fill, two of which—flooding in areas not filled above high tide and rotting foundation pilings of houses built on fill— are discussed in this book.

The walks in this book explore landmaking in various sections of the city. Each walk generally begins with the earliest filling in that area and then traces where and why subsequent landmaking took place. It is this emphasis on landmaking that differentiates this book from all the other walking tour books of Boston. Only in this book can you trace the topographical expansion of a given area, see your walk route on historical as well as current street maps, and compare historical views and photos with the present view from the same vantage point.

This book of walking tours is an outgrowth of and companion to my recent volume, *Gaining Ground: A History of Landmaking in Boston* (Cambridge, Mass.: MIT Press, 2003), which has a chapter on each section of Boston where there is made land. That book informs the walking tours I occasionally conduct, but was not so easy for others to use when exploring Boston's made land—though handsome, it's a hefty tome and several people commented that what they really needed was a book easier to carry around. At least one of these comments was made just when I was setting up walking tours for the class about Boston's landmaking that I periodically teach at the Harvard University Extension School and then the idea struck—I should write a book of walking tours to accompany *Gaining Ground*. And so was born *Walking Tours of Boston's Made Land*.

As you go around Boston on these walks, you may wonder how Bostonians managed to fill such vast areas. The answer is by employing a very simple method: they built a structure—during most of the 1800s usually a stone seawall—on the flats around the outer perimeter of an area to be filled and then simply dumped fill inside the structure until the level of fill was above the level of high tide. So I call it landmaking since that's what they were doing—making land by filling tidal flats—*not* landfill—since it was water that was being filled, not land—*nor* land reclamation—since the process did not involve diking, pumping, or draining to reclaim land from the sea. And, as you've noted, I refer to the product of this process as made land, *not* landfill.

Whatever the terminology or method of landmaking, however, the fact remains that Boston has a tremendous amount of made land, much of it in places that are not well known. So, choose an area you want to explore and start walking in order to learn how the land under your feet was made!

Members of The MIT Press enjoy a walking tour
conducted by Nancy S. Seasholes

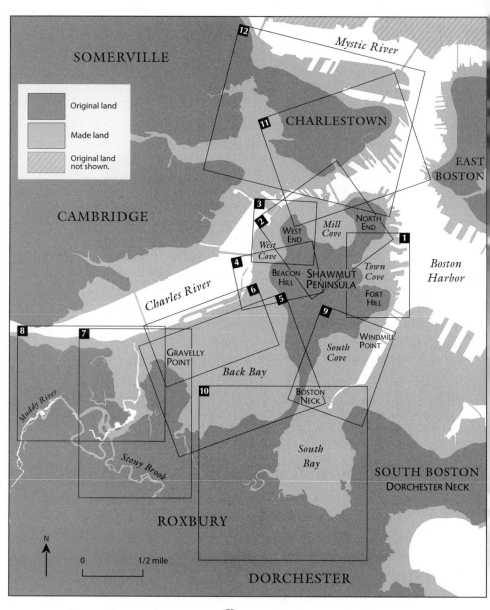

How to Use This Book

The following features are designed to help you navigate your way along the twelve walking tours presented in this book.

Key Map

The key map on the opposite page shows the location of each of the twelve areas covered in these walks.

Current Maps

Each walk is accompanied by its own map that plots the route of the walk on a current street map of that section of the city. On these current street maps, the start of the walk is marked by a number "1" in a square box, and the end is also indicated by a number in a square. Since all walks are designed to be accessible from Boston's subway system—known familiarly as the "T"—the name and location of the T station(s) closest to the start and finish of a walk is also indicated on the maps as well as specified in the text. (Other T stations in that area are shown but not labeled.)

Tour routes

The tour routes are marked on the maps in a heavy dark line with arrowheads, markings that should enable you to navigate the routes successfully despite Boston's notorious lack of street signs. (Note that the maps show all the streets in a given area, though label only those referred to in the text.) Since most of the walks attempt to trace the landmaking in a given area chrono-logically, that is, from the earliest to the latest, the route sometimes criss-crosses back and forth across that area. Numbers along the tour routes correspond to numbers in the margins of the text next to the relevant walk-ing directions (see below). Optional detours, which are explained below, are indicated on the maps with dashed lines. Bus routes, which are occasionally suggested (see below), are marked with dotted lines, and the one car route (see below) with a dashed and dotted line.

Walking Directions

The walking directions for each tour are in boldface type in the text. Usually the directions simply explain how to get from where you are to the next num-bered location on the map, but sometimes the directions are interspersed with comments in regular type about things you'll see along the way. Each direc-tion has a number in the margin that corresponds to a number on the current street map for that walk, as explained above. Often these numbers indicate stops—places where you should pause and read the information that follows in the text. But sometimes, especially when the directions send you along a street without specifying a stopping point, the information following the direction is intended to be read as you go along that street. Occasionally the directions suggest an optional detour to a place that is related to the land-making in that area. And in several instances, usually when the distances to be covered between stops are large, a public bus or, in one case, a car is recommended.

PRACTICAL INFORMATION

As a further aid to navigating the walks, the distance, time, location of public rest rooms, and any walking difficulties are listed at the beginning of each. Note that the distances have been measured but the times are approximate—those given are an average between fast and more leisurely walkers—and that these times are determined more by the number of stops on a given walk than its distance.

ILLUSTRATIONS

To help you follow progress of landmaking in the section of the city you're exploring, the walks are illustrated with historical maps, drawings, and photographs. On the historical maps, the walk route is sometimes marked with numbers corresponding to those on the current street map, so that you can compare the historical locations with the present ones. For the historical views and photographs, directions are included, where possible, to help you line up and compare those views with the present view from the same vantage point. And although existing buildings mentioned in the text are marked on the maps, current photos are sometimes included to help you identify them.

CROSS-REFERENCES

Some of the information and illustrations in this book are relevant to more than one walk. Sometimes such information is repeated in each walk to which it is germane, but more often the material is included in one walk and referred to in the others with page numbers and a ◆ next to the material in question. And for the sources of most of the information in the book, one should consult the relevant chapter, section, and reference notes in *Gaining Ground,* which is described in the Preface.

HISTORICAL MARKERS AND HARBORWALK

As you explore the city on these walks you will encounter numerous historical markers and plaques. The text directs you explicitly to some of these and, of the others, those in green installed by The Bostonian Society are generally the most accurate. Several of the walks follow HarborWalk, a continuous public walkway along the water's edge. HarborWalk can be identified by its distinctive blue and white signs and black iron railings. For more information about and maps of HarborWalk, consult its website:
http://www.bostonharborwalk.com.

SAFETY

Many of the walks in this book depart from the well-trod tourist trails and instead investigate less well known parts of the city. Boston is a relatively safe place to wander, but you will want to follow the usual precautions observed by city dwellers, from taking care when crossing streets to dressing down and wearing appropriate footwear to simply being constantly aware of your surroundings.

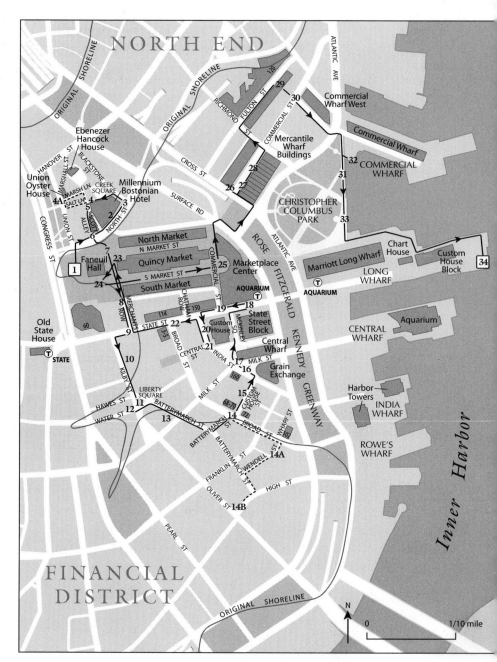

Current street map for Walk 1

Walk 1

CENTRAL WATERFRONT

Distance: 2 ¼ miles (including optional detours)
Time: 2 hours
Public Restrooms: Quincy Market building, Marriott Long Wharf

This walk traces the landmaking, or filling, that has taken place in Boston's central waterfront—an area that now includes Faneuil Hall and Quincy Market, much of State Street, the Custom House District, a small slice of the Financial District, and part of the North End. As you can see on the *key map,* what is now the central waterfront was once a large cove—known variously as the Town Cove, Great Cove, or East Cove—on the east side of the Shawmut Peninsula on which Boston was founded in 1630. And you can see on the *current street map* that the shoreline of the Town Cove was once far inland from its present location. Bostonians began to fill in the tidal flats in this cove in the 1630s and continued to do so until the present shoreline was reached in the early 1870s. (A little more filling was done a hundred years later in the early 1970s when Harbor Towers was built and Atlantic Avenue rerouted.) This walk will trace the progress of this landmaking in approximately the order in which it occurred. The route of the tour follows the shoreline in various time periods, attempting to remain on what was land at the time and not step into what was once water.

Start at the Sam Adams statue on the Congress Street side of Faneuil Hall.   1
Nearest T stops—State (Orange/Blue Lines), Aquarium (Blue Line), Government Center (Green/Blue Lines).

TOWN DOCK IN THE 1630S AND 1640S
As indicated on the *current street map*, the Sam Adams statue is almost at the head of the original Town Cove. Note that the 1630 shoreline of the cove is etched in the pavement near the statue with wavy lines interspersed with an occasional fish, feather, or the like—intended to depict the seaweed and other flotsam that would have marked the high tide line. The location of this shoreline is not entirely accurate, however, as you can see when you compare it with the 1630 shoreline marked on the *current street map*—the one in the pavement veers off toward Congress Street whereas the original shoreline actually ran toward North Street. (The rows of small rectangles etched in the pavement and the different colored granites are meant to depict street and wharf lines in this area in 1819.)

When the Puritans founded Boston in the 1630s, they settled first around the shores of the Town Cove and the North End, so it is not surprising that the   ♦
earliest landmaking occurred here. In the 1630s Bostonians began to fill in and

straighten the shores at the head of the cove—approximately on either side of today's Faneuil Hall (*see current street map*)—to make it easier for boats to land. This town landing place soon became known as the Town Dock—the origin of the name Dock Square later applied to this area (*see 1722, 1796, 1814, and 1852 maps*. Note that until the 1900s the term "dock" meant the *water* in an enclosed basin or a slip between wharves, *not* a structure at which ships moored.) By the 1640s Bostonians were also building wharves out into the Town Cove to serve the shipping on which the town's economy depended, eventually filling in the docks between the wharves and creating new land—a process known as "wharfing out." Most of the new land made in Boston in the 1600s and 1700s resulted from wharfing out.

2   **Cross North Street and go right toward Blackstone Street.**

Although North Street is on original land (*see current street map*), that land was marshy when Boston was established in 1630. The marsh was soon filled, however, and by the late 1640s some houses had been built on North Street. So, as you're going down North Street, imagine these houses on the left and the straightened shore of the Town Dock and wharves of the Town Cove on the right. When you get to Blackstone Street, the large open area beyond is the result of Boston's "Big Dig," a project that put an elevated highway underground and then tore down the overhead structure. Some of the newly created open space is now being developed as parks. (If it is a Friday or Saturday, Haymarket—Boston's open-air pushcart food market—will be in operation.)

3   **Stop at the corner of North and Blackstone Streets, facing up Blackstone toward the TD Banknorth Garden.**

MILL CREEK

In 1643 the town of Boston granted the large cove originally between the North and West Ends (*see map of made land*) to a group of proprietors (shareholders) on the condition that they build some grist mills for public use. The proprietors dammed off the cove to form the Mill Pond (see Walk 2, ♦ p. 32) and dug the Mill Creek to connect the pond and the harbor. At high tide water rushed from the harbor through the Mill Creek into the Mill Pond. As the tide fell, water in the Mill Pond was released, powering grist mills on the shore of the pond (about halfway down the new brick building beyond the one labeled "Pete's Pub"—*see current street map*) and rushing back through the Mill Creek to the harbor. The Mill Creek was on the line of present Blackstone Street and was apparently deep enough to be navigable, for deeds refer to its use by "boats, shallops, pinnaces, barks, ships, and sloops." There was a drawbridge over the Mill Creek on North Street.

4   **Go down Blackstone Street, take the first left, and follow the stone-paved roadway into Creek Square.**

SCOTTOW'S DOCK IN THE 1600S

Creek Square is on the site of Scottow's Dock (*see 1676 map*), one of the enclosed docks—docks surrounded by land—in colonial Boston. Enclosed docks were important in the 1600s because they provided protected anchorages for the small, shallow-draft ships of that period. Scottow's Dock was created in 1654 when Joshua Scottow dug out the marshy center section of what is today the Blackstone Block (the block bounded by Blackstone, North, Union, and Hanover Streets; *see current street map*). Ships entered Scottow's Dock from the harbor by going through the drawbridge on North Street, then sailed up the Mill Creek and into the dock—the same route you've just taken (*see 1676 map*).

Archaeologists found evidence of Scottow's Dock in 1981 during construction of the Bostonian Hotel—the building between where you are and North Street. The corner of a cobb wharf—a wharf constructed of timbers built up log-cabin style and the interior filled with rocks—was unearthed projecting from the vicinity of the present iron chain fence into the area where cars now park. These wharf remains may have been preserved by a 1706 agreement stipulating that no buildings should ever be erected on this area. Deeds indicate that in the 1600s there were warehouses along the west side of Scottow's Dock—where the roadway now runs behind the buildings on Union Street.

1676 map

Creek Square is also notable because it is one of the few places in modern Boston where one can get a sense of the colonial town. Salt and Marsh Lanes, the streets running between the square and Union Street, date from the 1600s (*see 1676 map*) and are about the same width as streets of that period. And the view north-ward from the square toward the 1767 Ebenezer Hancock House (*photo*)—the three-story brick building with a slate hip roof, which was built in 1767 by a brother of John Hancock—is essentially a 1700s streetscape. **To see more of the 1700s Blackstone Block, take the optional detour below. Otherwise, skip ahead to "Scottow's Dock in the 1700s."**

Ebenezer Hancock House

4A **Optional detour. Go up Salt Lane to Union Street and cross to the other side of Union in front of the Holocaust Memorial.**

Opposite you is the Union Oyster House, of which the older part (on the right) was built in 1716–1717.

Looking down Marshall Street to your left, you can see the Boston Stone (behind the two white-topped black stanchions) embedded in the wall of the building across from the Ebenezer Hancock House. The Boston Stone was *not* the stone from which distances on Boston-area milestones were measured, as many think, but rather a stone used in the late 1600s to grind paint pigments. In 1737 the stone trough of the paint grinder was set in the wall of the house then on the site to keep carriage wheels from hitting the building, and in 1835, when the present building was constructed, both the trough and the pestle—the round stone—were set in the wall of the new building.

4 **Return down Marsh Lane (next to 33 Union Street) to Creek Square.**

SCOTTOW'S DOCK IN THE 1700S

◆ Scottow's Dock was partially filled in the early 1700s. By that time enclosed docks were no longer in demand—ships were larger, had deeper drafts, and did not need protected anchorages. The north side of Scottow's Dock was filled in by 1706, leaving open only a narrow channel from the Mill Creek—approximately where the entrance roadway from Blackstone Street is today. The 1981 archaeological investigation found evidence of this filling on the north side of the original dock (*see 1676 map*)—dense concentrations of arti-facts, such as broken dishes and clay smoking pipes, dating from the late 1600s and early 1700s, which suggested that the dock was filled with whole cartloads of trash that were simply dumped into it. At almost the same time the dock was filled, in 1712 the drawbridge on North Street, which had become unsafe, was made a fixed bridge, preventing masted vessels from entering the dock. The filling of most of the dock and its closure to many vessels is probably why it was not labeled on a famous 1722 map of Boston (*see 1722 map*) or on subsequent maps. Scottow's Dock was then completely forgotten and only rediscovered in 1981 through the research for the archaeological investigation of the Bostonian Hotel Site.

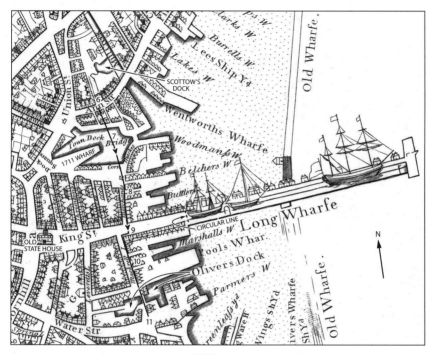

1722 map

Facing in the direction of North Street, bear right past Salt Lane and stop in front of the landscaped garden behind a wrought iron fence and gate. 5

An archaeological investigation here in 1983 found a saw pit, cistern, drains, and privies—typical of the 1600s, 1700s, and 1800s infrastructure that underlay Boston until modern construction destroyed most of it.

From the wrought iron fence go straight ahead toward North Street through a gate into Scott (*sic,* should be Scottow's) Alley, a *very* narrow passage. 6

Scott (*sic*) Alley is a right-of-way that dates from the 1600s (*see 1676 map*). When you emerge on North Street, turn and note the name chiseled over the entrance to the alley.

7 **Cross North Street and stop at the head of North Market Street, which runs between the North Market and Quincy Market buildings.**

TOWN DOCK IN THE 1670S

Since the walking tour last visited the area of the Town Dock, as it was in the 1640s, by the 1670s it had been completely enclosed by landmaking around its mouth (*see 1676 map*). Ships entered the dock through a "swing" bridge—so-called be-cause it pivoted to open—approximately on today's North Market Street. As you cross North Market Street, note that you are crossing the open water of the Town Dock—where Faneuil Hall is today (one of the few times this on this walk when you do "step in the water")—and that the swing bridge would have been down the street to your left (*see 1676 and 1722 maps*).

8 **Go between the market buildings and Faneuil Hall and go down Merchants Row.**

Merchants Row was the closest street to the water in the early 1700s. As you go down it, think land to the right and wharves to the left (*see 1722 map*).

9 **Cross State Street and stop opposite Merchants Row.**

OLD STATE HOUSE

State Street—called King Street until its name was understandably changed after the American Revolution (*see 1722 map*)—was the main drag from the harbor into the town during the first centuries of Boston's existence (*see 1676 and 1722 maps*). A town house built in 1657 at the head of King Street was replaced in 1713 by the Old State House (*photo*)—adorned with the lion and the unicorn of the English throne—the place where the General Court (the Massachusetts legislature), the Governors Council, and Boston's town meeting met (the last only until 1742, when it moved to the newly completed Faneuil Hall). The Old State House is in the middle of State Street today because that is where it was located historically (*see 1722 map*).

Old State House

BARRICADO

The first major landmaking in the Town Cove was the building of a barrier across the entire mouth of the cove in the 1670s to protect Boston against an attack from Dutch fire ships—old ships set ablaze and then set drifting toward an enemy's ships and wharves. As an English colony, Boston was always subject to attack by England's enemies, and in the 1670s England was at war with Holland. The barrier, appropriately named the Barricado, was built of branches, stones, and timbers by a group of proprietors approximately on the line of later Atlantic Avenue (beyond where traffic is crossing at a stoplight far down State Street) and is shown on the *1722 map* as the "Old

Wharfe." A few gaps were left in the Barricado so that friendly ships could reach the wharves in the Town Cove but, to compensate the wharf owners for the inconvenience, they were allowed to extend their wharves out as far as an imaginary *circular line* drawn three hundred feet from shore. The circular line intersected King (now State) Street at what is now Chatham Row—the street next to the gray eleven-story building that juts into State on the left as you look toward the waterfront *(photo)*.

LONG WHARF

The Barricado soon fell into disrepair—the propri-etors did not maintain it well and outgoing ships helped themselves to its stones for ballast. In 1707 the town began to receive proposals for a long wharf to be built out from the end of King Street, inter-secting the middle section of the Barricado and extending beyond it. The town approved such a wharf in 1710, primarily because it would facilitate repair-ing the Barricado. The real advantage of this long wharf, however, was that it would extend beyond the outer line of tidal flats, on which the Barricado was built, to deep water, enabling ships to load or unload directly onto the wharf without having to use small boats, or lighters, to ferry goods across the flats. As a

State Street narrowing at Chatham Row

condition of approval, the town required that King Street remain forever open its full width as far as the circular line, where Long Wharf began, and that is why today State Street narrows at Chatham Row *(photo)*. Long Wharf was built between 1711 and 1715. An archaeological investigation in the 1980s found that it was probably a crib wharf, that is, built up of timbers in log-cabin fash-ion—similar to a cobb wharf but without the interior rocks. Long Wharf extended almost a third of a mile into the harbor from the circular line *(see 1722 map)*—its end was at about the same place as at present.

Go up State Street toward the Old State House and turn left on Kilby 10
Street.
Mackerel Lane, now Kilby Street, was the closest street to the water in the 1700s *(see 1722 map)*—as you go down it, think land to the right and wharves to the left.

Stop in Liberty Square next to the statue. 11

OLIVER'S DOCK

Liberty Square—the triangle at the intersection of Kilby, Water, and Batterymarch Streets—is near the site of Oliver's Dock, another of the enclosed docks in colonial Boston. Oliver's Dock was created in the 1640s when a marshy inlet south of the Town Dock was excavated to provide a "harbor" and was named after Peter Oliver, who acquired most of the surrounding area in the 1650s and 1660s. Part of the dock lay between what are now Water and Hawes Streets (to the left and right of the 10 Liberty Square building; *see current street map*) and was reached through a drawbridge on what is now Kilby Street (*see 1676 map*). But by the 1720s most of the dock west of Kilby Street had been filled in (*see 1722 map*). The filling had been precipitated by the replacement of the drawbridge with a fixed bridge c. 1710 because the former had become unsafe, just as had befallen the drawbridge on North Street, thus making the dock west of Kilby Street inaccessible to masted vessels, again similar to what had transpired at Scottow's Dock. A small part of the dock west of Kilby Street was left open, however, because both a natural stream and a large underground drain emptied into it and, had it been completely filled, nearby cellars would have flooded. An archaeological investigation in 1987 in connection with the construction of the 75 State Street Building (the one with gold trim behind Liberty Square) found some timbers, probably from Poole's Wharf, which was on the north side of Oliver's Dock (*see 1722 map*).

LIBERTY SQUARE

Liberty Square was the site of the Stamp Act riots in 1765. In 1793, during a feast to honor the French Revolution, a liberty pole was erected in the square in memory of the pre-Revolutionary Boston riots, thus giving the square its name. The statue in the center commemorates the Hungarian Revolution of 1956, its smashed form recalling the suppression of that uprising.

12 **Cross Kilby Street to the northwest corner of Kilby and Water Streets and look down Oliver Street, the street on the right-hand side of the One Liberty Square building.**

FORT HILL

Between Liberty Square and the Fort Point Channel there was once a high glacial drumlin (a steep, smooth oval hill) known as Fort Hill—its crest, on the site of present International Place, was about forty feet above the present street level (about the height of the third-floor cornice on the building on the right past the one with red awnings that you see when looking down Oliver Street). In the 1600s and 1700s a fort was located on the summit, hence the name. The fort was taken down after the Revolution and replaced by a landscaped circle, which, with Bostonians' proclivity for naming any intersection a square, was designated Washington Square. In the early 1800s Fort Hill was a fashionable residential district, and wealthy merchants, such as some who had made a killing in the China Trade (see p. 13), built large mansions on the hill. But in the 1820s and 1830s these merchants moved away, many to newly fashionable residential neighborhoods such as Beacon Hill, which was being developed at that time. Their mansions were then acquired by institutions such as the Boston Athenaeum and what became the Perkins School for the Blind. But in the late 1830s and 1840s these institutions left, too, and the mansions were purchased by absentee landlords who, anticipating that land values would increase because of the proximity to the business district, let the houses deteriorate. Into this declining neighborhood poured Irish immigrants, fleeing the 1840s potato famine in Ireland. The mansions were subdivided into tiny living units, ramshackle housing was built on every available inch of open space, and habitations were tunneled back into the hill. With privies on upper levels draining down onto lower areas, buildings jammed together, and underground dwellings with no ventilation at all, it is not surprising that Fort Hill was the center of Boston's 1849 cholera epidemic.

In 1854 a group of businessmen proposed cutting down Fort Hill in the area bounded by Milk, Pearl, and Broad Streets (*see 1852 map*). Their ostensible

1852 map

purpose was to permit expansion of the business district, but certainly their hidden agenda was to initiate Boston's first slum clearance project. The businessmen's project never came to pass, however, and in 1865 the city proposed cutting just one street—now Oliver Street (*see current street and 1852 maps*)—through the hill as a municipal improvement. Although the businessmen foresaw that such a plan would not work because the sides of the cut would cave in, the city persisted and began cutting Oliver Street through the hill in 1866. By October 1867 the cut was so

1867 photo down Oliver Street from Milk Street

deep that the city had to build a footbridge across it to enable schoolchildren who lived on the south side of the cut (on the right in the *1867 photo looking down Oliver from Milk Street*) to reach the school, which was on Washington Square on the north side (*see 1852 map*). Compare the 1867 view down Oliver Street and of the almost completed bridge (see *1867 photo looking down Oliver from Milk Street*) with the view down Oliver Street today, noting the height of the hill. (Another *1867 photo looking down Oliver Street*, which shows cutting down Fort Hill, is on p. 16 in the optional detour to Fort Hill—sections 14A and 14B below.)

Then in early 1868 it became apparent that the businessmen were right—the sides of the cut were caving in, nothing could be built near Oliver Street, and the whole hill would have to be taken down after all. The problem was that there was no place to put the dirt—it could not be taken to concurrent landmaking projects because it had a high clay content, precluding its use in raising the level of Bay Village (see Walk 5, ♦ pp.75–76) where good drainage was need, and was excluded by law from the South Boston Flats, which were required to be filled with material dredged from the harbor. So in 1868 cutting down Fort Hill ground to a halt. (To find out how the problem was resolved, see the section on Atlantic Avenue near the end of this walking tour, p. 27.)

13   Go down Batterymarch Street.

BATTERYMARCH
Batterymarch was the route taken by soldiers in the colonial era when marching from the Common to the South Battery (near present Rowe's Wharf), giv-

ing the street its name. The street ran next to the water, so, as you go down it, think steep bluffs of Fort Hill to your right and wharves to your left (*see 1796 map*).

At the corner of Batterymarch and Milk Streets, note the brick building with light stone trim on the far (southeast) corner and the good view down Milk Street of the west end of the Central Wharf buildings (the four-story brick building with a hip roof; see p. 17).

Take the first left after Milk Street—the section of Batterymarch that goes down to Broad Street—and stop at the corner of Batterymarch and Broad Streets, opposite Custom House Street. 14

BOSTON IN THE SECOND HALF OF THE 1700s/CHINA TRADE

By this point, the walking tour has traced much of the landmaking in Boston in the 1600s and 1700s—most of the land having been made by wharfing out or filling in enclosed docks (*see 1796 map*). Not much of this land had been made in the second half of the 1700s, however, which is not surprising given the state of Boston's economy during that period. In 1740 Boston was the colonies' leading port and shipbuilder and, with a population of about 17,000, the most populous in North America. But then the economy stagnated and the population began to decline; Boston was overtaken first by Philadelphia and then New York. There were various reasons for this economic downturn, among them that Boston had a currency crisis in the 1740s and, as the major British port closest to French Canada, suffered more from the mid-century wars between England and France than did other British North American towns. Then in the 1760s and early 1770s the town was preoccupied with the political unrest that preceded the Revolution. During the war Boston was occupied by the British, who, when they evacuated, left the town with many damaged buildings and a population of only 2,719. Recovery after the war was slow—the loss of trade with the West Indies and the flooding of the market with English goods caused severe depressions.

About 1790, however, stimulated in part by the inauguration of Boston's trade with China, the economy began to revive. The China Trade was three-cornered—New England ships took goods such as clothing and metal tools around Cape Horn to the Pacific Northwest (today's Washington, Oregon, and British Columbia) and traded them there to the Native Americans for sea otter pelts. The ships then carried the furs to China, where they were exchanged for tea, porcelains, and silks, and then transported the Chinese goods around the Cape of Good Hope at the southern tip of Africa—hence circumnavigating the globe—to New England. The China Trade was enormously profitable for participating merchants and brought new prosperity to Boston. Many people were attracted to the thriving town—Boston's population, which had crept back up to about 18,000 in 1790, almost doubled by 1810—creating a need for more land. Bostonians never considered expanding to the mainland at this time, however; instead, they solved the problem by filling in the tidal flats surrounding the peninsula to *make* more land. In the central waterfront, the locus of the town's maritime economy, land was made to provide new commercial facilities.

INDIA WHARF/BROAD AND INDIA STREETS

The first of these projects that created land for new commercial facilities was the famous India Wharf development. Organized by Uriah Cotting, who initiated many of Boston's early 1800s landmaking projects, India Wharf was a speculative venture by a small group of proprietors. In 1803 they contracted to have a stone seawall built to enclose a new wharf extending from the flats at Wendell's Wharf (*see 1796 map*) out to deep water and then, once the area enclosed was filled, to have brick commercial buildings designed by architect Charles Bulfinch erected on the made land. The project also involved filling a new, wide street, appropriately named Broad Street, over wharves and docks south of State Street to connect State with the former Batterymarch and then creating a second new street, named India Street after the new wharf, parallel to Broad Street to connect India and Long Wharves (*see 1814 map*). After the area between Broad and India Streets was filled, brick commercial buildings, also designed by Bulfinch, were constructed on the new land.

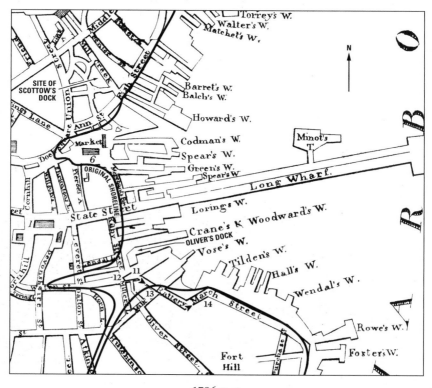

1796 map

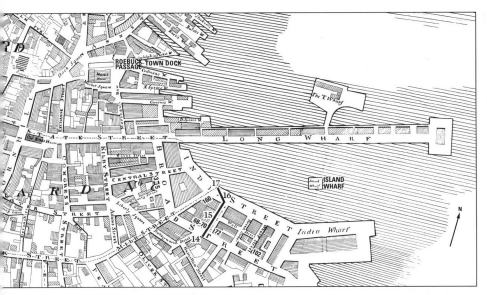

1814 map

India Wharf is now the site of Harbor Towers (*see current street map*). The main India Wharf Building has been demolished, but some of the other Bulfinch-designed buildings from the project still stand on Broad Street— the two at 64, 68–70 on the northwest corner of Custom House Street (*photo*); the one across from it at 72 Broad Street (*photo*), which is now virtually enveloped by the high-rise around it; and the one with shutters further down Broad Street at no. 102 on the corner of Wharf Street (*photo*). They are indicated on an *1814 map* of Boston—the first to show every structure in the town (parallel shading denotes brick buildings)—which also clearly shows, when compared with the *1796 map*, the amount of land made by the India Wharf/Broad and India Streets projects.

To see sites on the former Fort Hill (discussed on pp. 10–12), take the optional detour below. Otherwise, skip ahead to 15.

India Wharf buildings
at 64, 68–70 Broad Street

India Wharf building
at 72 Broad Street

India Wharf building
at 102 Broad Street

14A Optional detour. Go down Broad Street and turn right between the buildings at 99–105 and 109–139 Broad into the alley-like Wendell Street opposite the Bulfinch building at 102 Broad Street.

Wendell Street is on the site of Half Moon Place (*see 1852 map*), a nineteenth-century cul-de-sac that embodied all the worst living conditions on Fort Hill (see p. 11) and was featured in an 1849 city report on the cholera epidemic. Compare the present view up Wendell Street with the *view of Half Moon Place* from the 1849 report.

1849 view of Half Moon Place

14B Continue up to the end of Wendell Street at Batterymarch Street, go left on the latter to High Street, turn right and go down to the northeast corner of High and Oliver Streets.

This corner is approximately the site from which a *1867 photo looking down Oliver Street* with the bridge in the foreground was taken. The figures next to the bridge give an idea of the depth of the cut for Oliver Street. Compare this view with the present view, noting the height of Fort Hill, and with the *1867 photo down Oliver Street from Milk Street* on p. 12.

1867 photo down Oliver Street

Return to the corner of Broad and Batterymarch Streets either on   14
Batterymarch, on Oliver and Franklin Streets, or by retracing your
steps (*see current street map*).

From the corner of Broad and Batterymarch Streets, cross Broad Street   15
and go down Custom House Street.

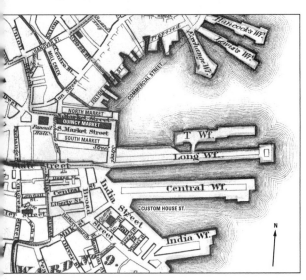

1826 map

The building at 20 Custom House Street is on the site of a custom house designed by Uriah Cotting and built in 1810 as part of the Broad/India Streets project, giving this street its name (*see 1826 map*). This custom house was the one in which author Nathaniel Hawthorne worked in 1839–1840 as a measurer of coal and salt.

**Stop at the triangle in   16
front of the Grain Ex-
change Building.**

CENTRAL WHARF

Following the India Wharf development, the next major commercial facility constructed on the central waterfront was Central Wharf, masterminded by Uriah Cotting and built in 1815–1816 between Long and India Wharves over a remaining piece of the Barricado (the "Island Wharf"; *see 1826 and 1814 maps*). Once the stone perimeter wall of Central Wharf had been constructed and the interior filled, a row of fifty-four attached three-bay-wide brick stores (warehouses) was built the length of the wharf. Of these original Central Wharf buildings (*photo*), only the westernmost nine still remain on Milk Street

Central Wharf buildings

next to the Grain Exchange Building (some were demolished in the early 1870s for Atlantic Avenue, some in the 1950s when the Central Artery was built, some in the 1960s in advance of the Aquarium, and some in the 1970s when Atlantic Avenue was relocated). The eastern part of Central Wharf is now the location of the Aquarium; for a sense of the wharf's original length, look down Milk Street toward the Aquarium.

Between the Central Wharf buildings and India Street is the Grain Exchange Building (*photo*), which is triangular because it is on land made by filling in the triangular dock between Central and India Wharves (*see 1852 map*) after Atlantic Avenue was built across the waterfront in 1869–1872 (see pp. 27–28).

17 **Cross the street to the northeast corner of India and Milk Streets (at the end of the Central Wharf buildings).**

From here you have a good view of the Grain Exchange building. Note the building across from you at

160 Milk Street—on the southwest corner of India and Milk Streets (*photo*)— which is clearly one of the Bulfinch-designed buildings for the Broad and India Streets project (compare it with those on Broad Street, described on p. 15, and *see 1814 map*). Looking up Milk Street toward the brick building with light stone trim that you passed on Batterymarch Street will help you visualize the amount filled to this point by 1808. The original shoreline was approximately at Batterymarch Street, now the far side of the brick building (*see current street map*); by the end of the 1700s wharfing out had filled to about what is now the middle of that building (*see 1796 map*);

Grain Exchange building

India Wharf building at 160 Milk Street

and from 1805 to 1808 the Broad and India Streets project created all the land between that point and where you are now on India Street (*see 1814 map*).

18 **Cross McKinley Square, cross State Street to near the T sign, and face back toward the Custom House.**

CUSTOM HOUSE

In the 1830s Boston's overseas shipping was at its height—Boston ships brought hides from California and South America for the growing Massachusetts shoe industry; cotton from the South for New England and British textile mills; wool from Australia and South America for New England woolen mills; tea from China (although this trade was increasingly centered in New York); coffee from Brazil; fruits, wine, and olive oil from the Mediterranean; and hemp and iron from the Baltic; and they took ice to the South, Caribbean, and India. To handle this volume of trade, in the 1830s the federal government decided to build a new custom house in Boston to replace the one built in 1810 on Custom House Street. The site of the new custom house was to be at the head of the dock between Long and Central Wharves.

In 1837 the government purchased the site, filled it (*see 1826 and 1852 maps*), and during the next ten years constructed the Custom House on the made land (*photo*).

As you can see from a *c. 1850 photograph*, the Custom House was originally two stories and surmounted by a dome; the tower was added in 1913–1915 as Boston's first skyscraper. In the *c. 1850 photo*, note the dock in front of the Custom

c. 1850 photo of Custom House

House and the bowsprit of a ship in it—a dock that was once right across from where you are now (*see 1852 map*).

There is an observation deck at the top of the Custom House with excellent views of the central waterfront. The observation deck can be visited—weather permitting—as part of daily tours of the Custom House, Monday–Friday at 10 AM and 4 PM and Saturday at 10 AM or on Sunday by

Custom House

special arrangement (617-310-6300). Or to see the interior of the original dome, enter the ground floor lobby from McKinley Square and look up through the circular opening in the center of the ceiling.

Go to the corner of State and Commercial Streets, the latter opposite the Custom House. Stop here and look back to view the facade of the State Street Block (the name is chiseled above the third floor), which is now One McKinley Square. **19**

State Street Block

STATE STREET BLOCK

By the 1850s the docks between the wharves on the central waterfront were too narrow for the larger, steam-powered ships then being built, so, with their commercial usefulness decreased, these docks began to be filled in. In the area where you are now, half of the dock between Long (now State Street) and Central (now Central Street) Wharves was filled in 1856–1857 (the dock shown in the *c. 1850 photo of the Custom House*) and the State Street Block (*photo*) was constructed on the made land.

The State Street Block used to be more than twice as long as it is now—it extended as far as the present eleven-story building near the water. The middle section of the State Street Block was demolished in the 1950s for the Central Artery and the eastern end was cut off in the early 1970s when Atlantic Avenue was moved further west.

20 Continue up State Street, at India Street (on the west side of the Custom House) cross to the opposite side of State, and go down India Street far enough so that, when you turn around, you have a good view of the building at 150 State Street (*photo*), including its roof.

150 State Street

Since the building at 150 State Street is east of Chatham Row (the former circular line), it is on what was Long Wharf and, with its narrow, four-story profile and gable roof, looks very much like the Long Wharf warehouses shown in a *1743 view* of Boston. (Don't be misled by the half-timbering and the dormer, which were installed in 1918, probably because the building was about to become the British Consulate.) Research conducted for this book, however, has established

1743 view of Long Wharf

that although the building is on the site of store (warehouse) no. 3 on Long Wharf, the original Long Wharf building was replaced when the present building was constructed sometime between 1826 and 1836.

Continue further down India Street to Central Street. 21

Central Street is where the entrance to Oliver's Dock was located (*see 1796 and 1814 maps*).

India Wharf Buildings at 3 and 5 Broad Street

Return to State Street, turn left, and go to the east corner of State and Broad Streets. 22

As you go up State, note the Old State House in its historic location in the middle of the street. Against the modern buildings behind it, it is a wonderful juxtaposition of Boston old and new. At the corner of State and Broad Streets, note 3 and 5 Broad Street (*photo*), which are Bulfinch-designed buildings in the Broad/ India Streets project (*see 1814 map*). The gray building with arched windows on the other side of State Street at no. 114, the Richards Building (1860s), is quite unusual in Boston, for it has a cast-iron facade. Mid-1800s buildings with cast-iron facades are common in many American cities but not Boston, probably because of the tradition here of constructing with granite.

Continue up State, turn right down Merchants Row, and go straight ahead to the steps on the far (north) side of the Quincy Market building. 23

TOWN DOCK IN THE 1700S/FANEUIL HALL

When the walking tour last visited the Town Dock area, as it was in the 1670s, it was an open body of water enclosed by made land (*see 1676 map*). In the 1700s, the Town Dock itself was filled in various stages for the same reasons as were the other enclosed docks in Boston—ships of that era were too large for these small, shallow anchorages and the docks had become polluted. In the case of the Town Dock, in 1711 the town built a wharf out into the dock from the southwest corner (*see 1722 map*) and in 1728–1729 filled the entire southern half of the dock. The fill, which archaeologists found when excavating under Faneuil Hall in 1990, contained broken wine bottles and glasses, clay smoking pipes, broken dishes, and shoes and shoe leather— apparently trash collected from nearby taverns, houses, and craft shops, just as had been used to fill Scottow's Dock in the same period (see p. 6).

The town then proposed erecting a public market on the newly made land. Bostonians had always been opposed to public markets, however, because they feared that dealers would buy up goods from farmers be*fore* the latter reached the market *stalls* and then charge any price they, the dealers, wanted—a practice

◆

1789 engraving of Faneuil Hall

known as forestalling. Nevertheless, in 1734 the town did build a public market on the made land at the Town Dock. It was not a success, however, for, driven by the antipathy to public markets, a mob tore it down one night in 1737. Then, in 1740 a Huguenot immigrant named Peter Faneuil offered to build his adopted town a new public market at his own expense. The town meeting still had to accept the gift, however, and, because of the opposition to public markets, only approved the proposal by seven votes out of over seven hundred. But approve it they did and the new market building was built at the Town Dock between 1740 and 1742 and promptly named Faneuil Hall in honor of its benefactor.

The north side of the Town Dock still remained open, however. But despite the fact that the dock was obnoxiously polluted—a 1744 visitor to the

1824 engraving of Faneuil Hall

town called it "a very stinking puddle"—and many proposals were made to fill it, the town did not actually fill the north side of the Town Dock until 1784, creating the land now occupied by the greenhouses. A *1789 engraving of Faneuil Hall* shows this newly made land on the north side of Faneuil Hall—the railings were for vendors to tie their horses to on market days. You may observe that Faneuil Hall looks much smaller in the 1789 engraving than it does today. That is because it was greatly enlarged in 1805 by architect Charles Bulfinch, who doubled its width and added a third story. An *1824 engraving of Faneuil Hall* plots the profile of the original Faneuil Hall on the 1805 building, clearly showing the extent of the enlargement.

Before leaving this location, note that the north wall of the Quincy Market building is aligned with the north wall of Faneuil Hall.

With Faneuil Hall on your right, cross diagonally in front of it and go straight ahead to the steps of the 60 State Street building. Turn to face Quincy Market.   24

FANEUIL HALL (QUINCY) MARKET

In 1822 Boston adopted a city form of government. Up until that time it had had a town meeting government, but with a population in 1820 of over 40,000, of whom more than 7,000 were voters, there were far too many to fit into the upper room in Faneuil Hall, where the town meeting met. Actually, town meetings were usually very poorly attended and operated without fiscal responsibility: taxes were set and approved by the same committees that expended the funds. These problems had been apparent for some time and proposals to change the town government had been introduced periodically since 1784, but none was approved until 1822. The new city government was headed by a mayor, who served a one-year term, and had a city council, composed of a board of aldermen and a common council.

The second mayor, Josiah Quincy, decided that a fitting project for the new city would be to clean up the old market area around Faneuil Hall—shown on the *1814 map*—and create a grand new marketplace. As shown on an *1823 plan*, the project involved constructing a seawall on the flats on the east line of what became Commercial Street, filling in the intervening old docks and wharves, and then erecting three new market buildings on the made land.

It was originally planned that the center market building—now called Quincy Market—be aligned with the center of Faneuil Hall. But the heirs of the Nathan Speare estate refused to sell their property to the city and, since it was right in the middle of the project (*see 1823 plan*), the project's southern boundary was moved northward and the north wall of Quincy Market was aligned with the north wall of Faneuil Hall. Then, after the cellar walls of the Quincy Market building had already been constructed, the Speare heirs decided to sell to the city after all, enabling the project to be extended south to Butler's Row (*see 1823 plan*), as originally intended. This meant that South Market Street would be widened to 102 feet while North Market Street,

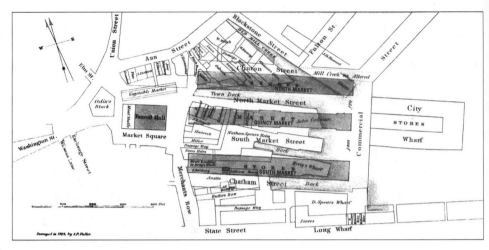

1823 plan of Faneuil Hall (Quincy) Market project

which had been narrowed when the Quincy Market building was moved northward, would be only 65 feet wide. People who had bought stores in the projected North Market building protested and, after considering the matter, the city council proposed that the North Market building owners could pay to move and entirely rebuild the cellar of the Quincy Market building so that it would be centered on Faneuil Hall. Almost needless to say, the North Market owners decided to leave the Quincy Market building where it was, and that is why today South Market Street is so much wider than North Market Street (*see 1823 plan*).

The project was carried out between 1824 and 1826, creating new land on which were built what are now called the Quincy Market and North and South Market buildings (*see 1823 plan and 1826 map*). These buildings became the center of Boston's food market district and remained so until the 1950s. In the 1960s the city decided to rehab the market buildings and they reopened on August 26, 1976—the 150-year anniversary of their original opening. And in observance of its original function, the Quincy Market building is still devoted to the sale of food.

25 Go back toward Quincy Market and down South Market Street (between the Quincy and South Market buildings) to Commercial Street (at the end of the market buildings).
Compare the view of the east end of the market buildings with the *1827 view* of them—the Marketplace Center building is obviously on made land. Also note the good view of the 1837–1847 Custom House and the tower. When the latter was added in 1913–1915, there was a 125-foot height restriction in Boston but, because it was a federal building, the Custom House tower was exempt. It was Boston's first skyscraper and remained the city's tallest building until the Prudential Building was constructed in 1964 in Back Bay.

1827 view of Faneuil Hall Market

Go left on Commercial Street, cross the Surface Road, take the walkway   26
toward Mercantile Mall, turn left on Cross Street (along the end of
Mercantile Mall), and go to the far side of the next corner (Commercial
Street).

You are now in the North End section of the city, one of the oldest sections of
Boston and the home successively of Yankees, Irish, Jews, and, since the
beginning of the 1900s, Italians. Though the North End is now being gentrified and Italians are no longer the majority, the Italian presence is still very
strong.

On the opposite side of Commercial
Street are the Mercantile Wharf
Buildings (see name chiseled above the
third story; *photo*), which were erected
in 1856 on land made by filling the
docks in front of Commercial Street (*see
1852 map*)—part of the same filling of
docks on the central waterfront that
created the land for the State Street
Block (see p. 19). The structure has a
plural name because each three-bay
section was sold as a separate building.
The western end was cut off in 1933
when Cross Street was widened to create an access route to the Sumner
Tunnel, which opened in 1934.

Mercantile Wharf Buildings

27 **Cross back across Commercial Street to the corner next to the Mercantile Wharf Buildings.**

COMMERCIAL AND FULTON STREETS

Commercial Street buildings

As a spin-off of the Faneuil Hall (Quincy) Market project in the 1820s, the city decided to extend two new streets to the North End by filling flats, wharves, and docks north of the market area (*see 1826 map*), somewhat as Broad and India Streets had been filled south of the market area earlier in the century. This filling took place in the late 1820s, creating an extension of Commercial Street and Fulton Street parallel to it. Brick commercial buildings (*photo*) were then built in the 1830s on the made land. Although these buildings have now been converted to residences, they are a very well preserved example of 1830s Boston commercial architecture. Like the Mercantile Wharf Buildings, the western ends of these buildings were truncated in 1933 for the widening of Cross Street—note the chimney flues still visible on the end walls.

28 **Go up Commercial Street to Richmond Street.**
As you go up Commercial Street, note that you are on what was the shoreline in the 1830s, 1840s, and early 1850s (*see 1852 map*).

29 **Turn left on Richmond Street and right onto Fulton Street.**
Many of the buildings on Fulton Street were also erected in the 1830s after the street was filled. The metal stars between stories on some buildings are the end stops of tie-rods—iron rods that extend through the building from front to rear in order to provide structural support. On the left at 120 Fulton Street note the McLauthlin Building, which was built about 1853 for a company that manufactured safes and is now residences—a beautiful example of one of Boston's few cast-iron facade buildings (see the Richards Building at 114 State Street, p. 21).

30 **Opposite the McLauthlin Building, turn right into the passage under the building on Fulton Street and pass through to Commercial Street.**
Now you are back on the waterfront of the 1830s, 1840s, and early 1850s (*see 1852 map*). Ahead of you is the west end of the Commercial Wharf building (1832–1834)—one of the large granite wharves built on the North End waterfront in the 1830s and 1840s during the heyday of Boston's overseas shipping (see p. 18 and *1852 map*).

Cross Commercial Street, go down the street on the right side of the   31
granite Commercial Wharf West building, cross Atlantic Avenue, and
go down the walk in front of Christopher Columbus (Waterfront) Park
to the benches near the water.

ATLANTIC AVENUE

The final project that created the present shoreline of the central waterfront
was the filling of Atlantic Avenue across the docks and wharves on the waterfront between 1869 and 1872. The Atlantic Avenue project was precipitated
by Bostonians' concern throughout the 1800s that the city was losing shipping to New York. In the 1860s the accepted reason for this loss of shipping
was that it was difficult to ship freight through Boston because there was no
rail connection between the depots that served the railroads entering Boston

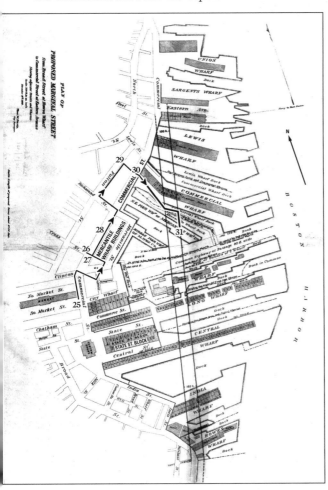

from the south,
which were located
in the Kneeland
Street area, and
those serving rail-
roads from the
north, which were
in the Causeway
Street area. The
proposed solution
was to lay a railroad
track on city streets
to connect the two
depot areas. The
original plan was to
put the track on
Broad, India, and
Commercial Streets
(*see 1852 map*), but
it then became clear
that building a new
street across the
waterfront would
shorten the route
(*see 1868 plan*).

1868 plan for Atlantic Avenue

The real impetus for the Atlantic Avenue project, however, was the Fort Hill project. As recounted on p. 12, cutting down Fort Hill had come to a halt in 1868 because there was no place to put the dirt. But it soon became apparent that if the Atlantic Avenue project were undertaken, the dirt from Fort Hill could be used to fill the docks that would be cut off by the new street (*see 1868 plan*). So in 1869 the Fort Hill project resumed and the Atlantic Avenue project got underway.

Building Atlantic Avenue involved not only filling across the docks on the central waterfront but also cutting through the buildings on the wharves (*see 1868 plan*). One example of a building separated by Atlantic Avenue still

exists: looking north, you will see the two parts of the Commercial Wharf building cut apart for Atlantic Avenue (*photo*), which is now the walkway next to the water in front of Christopher Columbus (Waterfront) Park. After Atlantic Avenue was completed in 1872, the tracks of the Union Freight Railroad were promptly laid on it and remained until 1970, when they were removed before Atlantic Avenue was relocated further west in the early 1970s. Thus, the historical line of Atlantic Avenue, which marks

Commercial Wharf building cut apart for Atlantic Avenue

the final landmaking in the central waterfront, is now delineated just by the walkways in front of Christopher Columbus (Waterfront) Park and between the Marriott Long Wharf and the Aquarium (*see current street map*).

The central waterfront remained a commercial area until the 1960s. Then, with the wharves no longer serving ships—many by then were used as parking lots—they began to be put to other uses. In the 1960s the Aquarium was built on Central Wharf. In the early 1970s Harbor Towers was built on India Wharf, Atlantic Avenue was rerouted west (both these projects involved a little more landmaking—*see current street map*), and Commercial Wharf and other granite wharf buildings in the North End began to be rehabbed as residences. In 1976 Waterfront (now Christopher Columbus) Park was created on the site of a former wholesale market building, and in the early 1980s the Marriott Long Wharf was built over part of Long and former T Wharves. So what was once the center of Boston's shipping has now been transformed into a vibrant residential and recreational area.

32   **Retrace your route on the walk next to the water as far as the restaurant, turn right onto HarborWalk, and go straight out to the end of the first section of the deck.**

From this point there is a good view of the seawall that was constructed for Atlantic Avenue.

Return down the walk by the water in front of Christopher Columbus **33**
Park, heading toward the Marriott.
The basin to your left, between Commercial and former T Wharves, was the home of the Boston fishing fleet from the 1880s until 1913, when it moved to the new Fish Pier in South Boston.

Just before the Marriott, turn left and follow HarborWalk out to the **34**
flagpole at the end of Long Wharf.
At the end of Long Wharf there is a historic view back into the city—down Long Wharf and up State (King) Street to the Old State House at the end. As

you return down Long Wharf toward the city, on the right you pass the Custom House Block (*photo*), built in the 1840s, and the Chart House (*photo*), which was begun in 1763 and added to in the 1820s.

Custom House Block

Chart House

This is the end of the walk. Nearest T stop—Aquarium (Blue Line).

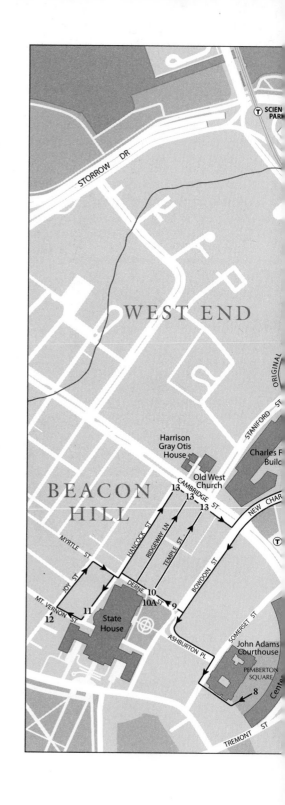

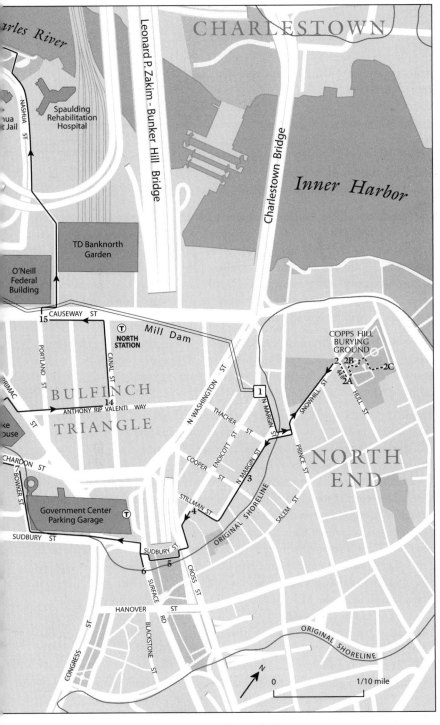

Current street map for Walk 2

Walk 2

BULFINCH TRIANGLE AND NORTH OF CAUSEWAY STREET

Distance: 3 miles (including optional detours)
Time: 1 3/4 hours
Public Restrooms: State House (security check; closed weekends), Adams Courthouse (security check; closed weekends), Brooke Courthouse (security check; closed weekends), Hurley Building (security check; closed weekends), O'Neill Federal Building (security check; closed weekends), North Station/TD Banknorth Garden
Note: This walk goes up and down several relatively steep hills.

This walk traces all the landmaking that has occurred in the large cove that was once between the North and West Ends (*see map of made land*). As you can see on the *current street map*, the walk explores parts of the North End and its densely packed nineteenth-century buildings, Beacon Hill with its charming nineteenth-century town houses, the Bulfinch Triangle and its handsome nineteenth-century commercial buildings, and the area north of Causeway Street, which includes a new park along the Charles River.

1 **Start at the bend in Endicott Street at the intersection of North Margin Street.**
Nearest T stop—North Station (Green and Orange Lines).

MILL POND
Between this point and the Charlestown Bridge, Endicott Street follows the original shoreline of the cove (*see current street map*) and the bend in the street marks the location of a dam that was once across the cove and of a mill powered by it. In the 1640s the town of Boston granted the whole cove to a group of proprietors (shareholders) on condition that they build some grist (flour) mills for use by the townspeople. The proprietors extended dams from both ends of a natural causeway that already existed across the mouth of the cove, damming off the whole cove, which then became known as the Mill Pond. At high tide water flowed into the pond through a floodgate in the dam here and through the Mill Creek on the site of today's Blackstone Street (*see current street map*). As the tide fell, water was released from the Mill Pond, powering mills here and on the south shore of the Mill Pond at a site you'll visit later on this walk.

By the end of the 1700s the Mill Pond had become very polluted by wastewater discharged from drains serving the surrounding houses and rum distilleries, by seepage from privies (outhouses), and by people disposing of dead animals by throwing them into the pond. The pollution was considered especially serious because at that time people thought diseases were caused by odors, or "miasmas," from rotting animal and vegetable matter—a belief known as the miasmatic theory of disease. In 1804 a new group of proprietors proposed filling up the Mill Pond and selling the resulting land for house lots. Boston needed more land at this time because the population was growing very rapidly (see Walk 1, ♦ p. 13), but the town nonetheless argued about the proposal for several years since to accept it meant giving up the public flour mills. Finally, in 1807 the town agreed that the Mill Pond could be filled, and the proprietors, who by then had been incorporated as the Boston Mill Corporation (BMC), began to fill in the pond.

Go down North Margin Street, turn left on Thacher Street to Prince Street, jog left on Prince and then right onto Snowhill Street. Go up Snowhill Street to Hull Street (at the top of the hill and next to Copps Hill Burying Ground).

You have been going through the North End section of Boston. The North End is one of the oldest neighborhoods of the city because it borders the Town Cove, where settlement first clustered, and because most of the North End is original land (*see map of made land* and Walk 1, ♦ p. 3). In the 1600s and 1700s the North End was populated by a mix of well-to-do merchants and town leaders, craftsmen such as Paul Revere, and laborers. In the early 1800s, however, many of the upper and middle class moved elsewhere and the North End quickly declined, the once-proud mansions either replaced by tenements or divided into rooming houses. Into this overcrowded neighborhood poured the Irish in the 1840s, fleeing the potato famine in Ireland. The Irish were the dominant group in the North End until the 1880s, when they were replaced first by Eastern European Jews, especially in the Salem Street area, and then by Italians. Other residents have now moved into areas being "gentrified" and Italians are no longer in the majority, but the North End still has a strong Italian presence.

FILLING THE MILL POND

The BMC began to fill the Mill Pond in 1807. Most of the fill was gravel from nearby hills and, in the early years of the project, much of this gravel came from Copps Hill—the hill you are now on. The height of the retaining wall on the right-hand side of Snowhill Street next to the Copps Hill Burying Ground (*photo*) indicates the amount of hill cut away for use as fill.

The gravel was then carted down the steep hill you have just climbed up and dumped into the Mill Pond.

To see what may be the narrowest house in Boston, Copps Hill Burying Ground, and good views of the Charlestown Navy Yard, *Constitution* **("Old Ironsides"), and the Bunker Hill Monument, take the optional detour(s) below. Otherwise, skip ahead to 3.**

Retaining wall on Snowhill Street

2A   Optional detour to what is reputedly the narrowest house in Boston. Turn right on Hull Street and go down to no. 44.

This house was traditionally thought to have been built about 1804. Research conducted for this book, however, has established definitively that the house was built in 1883–1884. (Its Italianate details—projecting tabbed window hoods, paired brackets, and a dentil course—which would be unusual on an 1880s house, were probably copied from the houses originally at 46 and 48 Hull Street, which were built in the 1860s.) This house was supposedly a "spite" house, built to block the side view from the house once at 46 Hull Street. But the recent research suggests that this house was built simply to create another saleable property on a lot that once included 46 and 48 Hull Street.

2B   Optional detour to Copps Hill Burying Ground. Enter the gate on Hull Street opposite the narrowest house, jog left, then turn right, go right halfway around the first circle, and continue to the next walk.

This is one of the oldest burying grounds in Boston—the town bought it in 1659. Reading both the plaques in the ground and the numbered historical markers, which are on the route described above, will give you information about it.

2C   Optional detour to views of the Charlestown Navy Yard, *Constitution* ("Old Ironsides"), and, to the left, Bunker Hill Monument. From the end of detour 2B, turn right (note another historical plaque to the right), then left at the next main walkway, and go about halfway down that walk.

These views are particularly good when there are no leaves on the trees.

2   At the end of any or all of these optional detours, return to the corner of Snowhill and Hull Streets.

3   From the corner of Snowhill and Hull Streets, retrace your route to the corner of Thacher and North Margin Streets. Turn left on North Margin Street.

As you go down North Margin Street, note that the original shoreline of the Mill Pond was to your left (*see current street map*) and you are on land made by the BMC between 1807 and 1809, all probably filled with gravel from Copps Hill. North Margin, Cooper, which you cross, and Stillman Streets were three of the first streets laid out on the newly made land in the Mill Pond.

4   At Stillman Street, turn right and go to Endicott Street.

Filling of Endicott Street began before that of the Mill Pond. In 1806, while the town was still considering whether to allow the Mill Pond to be filled, another group of proprietors got permission to fill a street across the pond in order to shorten the route from the Hanover Street area to the bridge to Charlestown (*see current street map*). The street, originally called Pond, or Mill Pond, Street was filled from 1806 to 1809 (*see 1807 map*).

1807 map

Turn left on Endi- 5
cott Street and at
the end bear left
onto Cross Street.
At Sudbury Street
cross Cross Street
(note the good view of
the Zakim Bridge),
turn left, and turn
right onto the walk-
way across the park.
This park is a prod-
uct of Boston's Big
Dig, a project in
which the elevated
highway through the
city was put under-
ground and then
parks such as this one
were laid out on top.
To your left was the
Mill Pond Site, an
archaeological site
excavated in 1993 before Big Dig construction began. Archaeologists found
evidence of landmaking in the early 1700s along the shore of the Mill Pond—
large criss-crossed timbers to retain fill had been laid down on the bottom of
the pond and fill then dumped on top of them. The line of granite stones in
the ground marks the line of a double wood bulkhead (wall), which the
archaeologists also found. This double bulkhead found archaeologically
turned out to be just where a double line is shown along the shore of the Mill
Pond on an *1814 map*. The town had probably built this bulkhead about
1771 to mark the boundary of its grant to the mill pond proprietors. The seg-
mented line shown around the shore of the Mill Pond on the *1807 map* also
probably represents the bulkhead. Read the signage about the bulkhead.

At the end of the walkway across the park turn right to Sudbury Street, 6
cross the Surface Road, turn left, and go to the upright millstone.
The line of granite stones in the brick sidewalk marks the west wall of the Mill
Creek, a waterway that once ran between the harbor and the Mill Pond, filling
the pond at high tide and emptying it at low. When the water rushed out of
the pond at ebb tide, it powered mills on the shore of the pond at the head of
the Mill Creek just a few feet from where you are. The millstone and parts of a
mill wheel were found in 1999 during Big Dig construction. Read the signs
about the Mill Creek wall, the millstone, and the workings of South Mill.

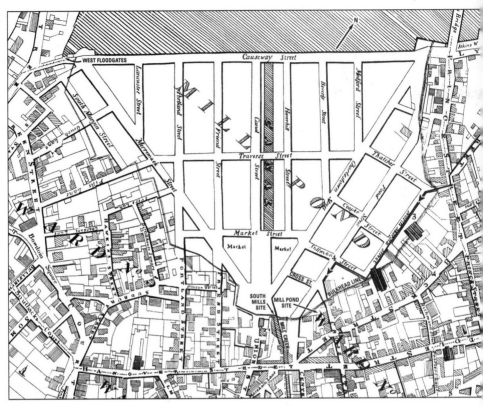

1814 map

7   Return to the corner of the Surface Road and Sudbury Street, cross and
    turn left on Sudbury Street (next to the Government Center parking
    garage), and go right on Bowker Street (the steps and street at end of
    parking garage) to New Chardon Street.
    You have been following the original shoreline of the Mill Pond (*see current
    street map*). The western part of the parking garage is on land made about
    1809 or 1810.

8   Turn left on New Chardon Street, go up to and cross Cambridge Street,
    go up Bowdoin Street (on the east [left] side for the best view of the older
    buildings on the west side of the street), turn left on Ashburton Place (on
    the far side of John W. McCormack Building), turn right on Somerset
    Street, turn left on the passage next to the old Suffolk County (John
    Adams) Courthouse, and go down the passage to Pemberton Square (the
    open area between the John Adams Courthouse and Center Plaza).
    From the steps in front of Center Plaza there is a good view of the facade of
    the old Suffolk County Courthouse (1896), which in 2002 was renamed the
    John Adams Courthouse.

Boston & Lowell Railroad Land

Pemberton Square is on the site of the easternmost peak of Beacon Hill, called
Pemberton Hill in the early 1800s. In 1835, the Boston & Lowell Railroad,
one of the first railroads to serve the city, hired an ox-drover (teamster) named
Asa Sheldon to cut down the hill and take the gravel to fill an area north of
Causeway Street for the railroad's depot. Sheldon accomplished this huge task
in just five months, using sixty-three teams of oxen to haul the fill and creating fourteen acres of new land. (You'll see the area he filled later on this walk.)

**Retrace your route as far as the northwest corner of Bowdoin and
Derne Streets.**

Filling the Mill Pond (Revisited)

Although some of the early fill for the Mill Pond came from Copps Hill (see
p. 33), most of the fill ultimately came from Beacon Hill. What we now call
Beacon Hill was originally a long glacial moraine with three separate peaks
called the Trimountain, a name that has survived in Boston as "Tremont."
The middle, and highest, peak had a beacon on its summit in the 1600s and
1700s and hence became known as Beacon Hill. In 1789 the beacon blew
down and in 1790 architect Charles Bulfinch replaced it with a columnar

monument surmounted
by an eagle to commem-
orate the Revolution.
The monument stood in
the middle of a ninety-
nine-foot-square lot the
town owned at the top
of the hill. The land surrounding it was owned
by the heirs of John
Hancock, who, in the
first years of the 1800s,
began to cut down the
hill, presumably so they
could sell the fill. An
1811 drawing of Beacon

**1811 drawing of Beacon Hill from
Bowdoin Street**

Hill from Bowdoin Street shows the results—the Hancocks' digging had caved
in the northeast corner of the town's land and undermined the foundation of
a house belonging to a Mr. Thurston to such an extent that it later had to be
taken down. Compare the *1811 drawing of Beacon Hill from Bowdoin Street* with
the present view (best done when the leaves are off the trees; note that you
may have to go into the street to line the views up correctly—use the cupola
of the State House in the 1811 drawing), observing the difference in the
height and location of the monument (the present monument is a replica
erected in 1898). This comparison indicates how much of Beacon Hill was cut

9

down (about sixty feet) and that the original summit was where the rear wing of the State House is now.

10   **Go down Derne Street to the corner of Temple Street.**
Another in the set of *1811 drawings of Beacon Hill*, this one of the hill *from Derne Street*, was made from this location. Compare it with the present view of the steps up to the State House, noting how steep the original hill was, that you can no longer see the cupola of the State House because it's obscured by the rear wing, the difference in location and height of the monument—again an indication of how much the hill has been cut down—and, on the *1811 drawing,* the northeast corner of the town's land cut away by the Hancocks next to Mr. Thurston's house.

1811 drawing of Beacon Hill from Derne Street

10A **For a short optional detour to read some historical markers, cross Derne Street.**
Read the historical markers on the wall about the site of the first English High School and the naming of Derne Street.

11   **Continue west on Derne Street, turn left on Hancock Street, and go almost to the corner of Mt. Vernon Street (so that the cupola of the State House is visible in the corner at the beginning of the rear wing).**
Compare this view with the *1811 drawing of Beacon Hill from the back of the State House* from about the same vantage point (align the cupola of the State House in both views). In 1811 the town decided to sell its lot at the top of Beacon Hill. It was purchased by none other than the Hancock heirs, who proceeded to cut down the hill in earnest. In the 1811 drawing you can see the excavation being done with hand tools—shovels and pick axes—and the gravel being loaded into horse-drawn tip carts, which were the standard means of transporting fill in the 1800s, to be taken down to the Mill Pond. People often think this *1811 drawing of Beacon Hill from the back of the State House* shows the front of the State House but, as you can see when you compare the locations of the cupola, the confusion is because the rear facade, now covered by the rear wing, was originally similar to the front. In the *1811 drawing of Beacon Hill from the back of the State House* you can also see the steeple of the recently completed Park Street Church (1810) at the corner of Park and Beacon Streets.

1811 drawing of Beacon Hill from the back
of the State House

Turn right on Mt. Vernon Street and go to the southeast corner of Mt.   12
Vernon and Joy Streets.
Compare this view with the *1811 drawing of cutting down Beacon Hill from Mt.*
Vernon Street from about the same place you are now. Again note the extent of
cutting down Beacon Hill, the use of hand tools and horse-drawn tip carts,
the original location of the summit, and Mr. Thurston's house in the distance.

1811 drawing of Beacon Hill from
Mt. Vernon Street

13 Go north on Joy Street to Myrtle Street, turn right, and go down either Hancock Street, Ridgeway Lane, OR Temple Street to Cambridge Street.

If you choose Hancock Street, note the green plaque on the house at no. 57 at the corner of Hancock and Derne Streets. The house at  the foot of Hancock Street on the far side of Cambridge Street is the first Harrison Gray Otis house (1796 [*photo*]; see Walk 3, ♦ p. 50). The church at the foot of Ridge-

Harrison Gray Otis House

way Lane on the opposite side of Cambridge Street is Old West Church (1806 [*photo*]; see Walk 3, ♦ p. 50).

Old West Church

Whatever street you chose, you have been going down the north slope of Beacon Hill, which is explained in Walk 4, ♦ p. 61.

14 Turn right on Cambridge Street, left on New Chardon Street, and go between the Edward W. Brooke Courthouse (on the right) and the Charles F. Hurley Building (on the left),** crossing the original shoreline (*see current street map*), **to Merrimac Street. Turn right on Merrimac and then left on Anthony Rip Valenti Way (formerly Traverse Street) to Canal Street.**

BULFINCH TRIANGLE

Since Merrimac Street, you have been going through the Bulfinch Triangle, the name now applied to the land created when the Mill Pond was filled. The name refers to the triangular street plan (*see 1814 and current street maps*), which was devised in 1808 by a committee of Boston selectmen of which architect Charles Bulfinch, who drafted the plan, was a member—hence the name. The triangular plan was probably determined by the pre-existence of diagonal Pond (Endicott) Street (see pp. 34–35 and *1807 map*).

♦   While the Mill Pond was being filled, a canal was constructed through it (*see 1814 map*) to fulfill an original requirement that the Mill Creek, which ran between the harbor and the Mill Pond on a route you crossed earlier in the walk, be continued to the Charles River. The canal, which was built in 1810–1813 by constructing seawalls on either side, was considered part of the Middlesex Canal, which itself had been constructed in 1794–1803 from Charlestown to the Merrimack River at what is now Lowell, Massachusetts. Canal boats used a system of bouyed cables to cross the Charles River between Boston and Charlestown when going to and from the terminus of the Middlesex Canal near today's Sullivan Square. In the Bulfinch Triangle, the

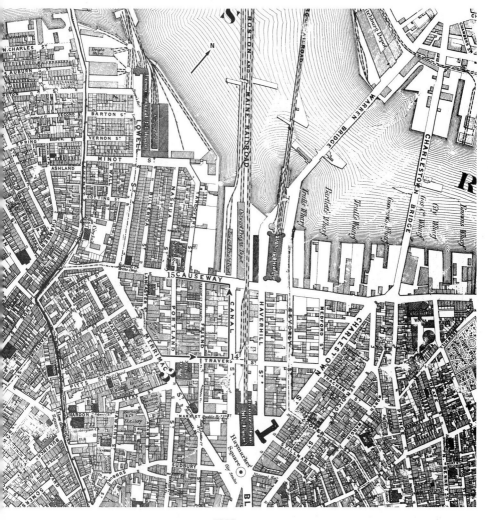

1852 map

canal ran along the eastern side of Canal Street, which is where you are now (*see 1814 map*).

The BMC finally finished filling the Mill Pond in 1828. The made land had been intended for residential use but, although some houses were initially built, particularly in the North End east of what is now North Washington Street, most of the triangle became industrial and commercial. In 1844 the canal down the center was filled in for the tracks of the Boston & Maine Railroad, which were laid in 1845 to a depot in Haymarket Square (now the location of the Haymarket T station; *see 1852 map*. In 1908 when the Green Line was being extended from Haymarket to North Station on this same alignment, remains of the canal walls were found during the excavation). The railroad attracted light industries; in 1867, for example, the blocks between

Haverhill and Beverly Streets (*see 1852 map*) were occupied by enterprises such as machine shops, blacksmiths, and marble works.

15   **Go left on Canal Street, turn left on Causeway Street, and go to Portland Street.**

CAUSEWAY STREET

Causeway Street delineated the northern extent of the Mill Pond project (*see 1814 map*). A seawall was built to form the north side of the street—from the west side of the Mill Pond to the canal in 1812–1815 and from the east side of the canal to Pond (now Endicott) Street in 1824–1826—replacing the dam across the Mill Pond (*see 1807 and 1814 maps*). The flats north of Causeway Street did not remain unfilled for long, however. As explained above, in 1835 the Boston & Lowell Railroad filled some of the flats with dirt from Pemberton Hill to make land for depots, land now occupied by the O'Neill Federal Building on the opposite side of Causeway Street. And other railroads that entered Boston from the north also filled flats north of Causeway Street for their depots, soon lining the north side of the street with railroad stations (*see 1852 map*). Most of these depots were consolidated in 1893 into a Union Station. It was replaced in 1928 by North Station, which stood on a site

1880s buildings on Portland Street

between Causeway Street and the present TD Banknorth Garden until it was demolished in 1998.

As for the Bulfinch Triangle, in the 1880s five- and six-story brick furniture factories and warehouses replaced most of the original structures. Some of these late-1800s buildings still exist and you can see them as you go down Causeway Street—a particularly good group stands on Portland Street, for example (*photo*).

16   **Cross Causeway Street and go down the entrance walkway to the TD Banknorth Garden/North Station. Go past the TD Banknorth Garden on your right, down the stairs, and follow the walkway to Nashua Street, the street on the left side of the Spaulding Rehab Hospital.** (Note the spectacular views to your right of the Zakim Bridge.) **After you pass Spaulding Rehab on the right, enter the Nashua Street Park and turn left to go along the river.**

LANDMAKING IN THE 1900s

Most of the land north of the TD Banknorth Garden was made in the late 1920s and early 1930s by the Boston & Maine Railroad. When the railroad built North Station in 1928 (see above), it received permission to fill a large area of flats behind the station so that passengers in rear cars of trains could disembark on solid ground instead of onto trestles. The landmaking project, which also involved filling on the other side of the river in Charlestown and Cambridge, actually began in 1927 and continued for several years. Seawalls were constructed on both sides of the river and the flats filled with dirt from a hill in Somerville, which was carried to the sites by rail, and with debris from several buildings in Boston that were being demolished at that time. The new land created is now the location of the Spaulding Rehabilitation Hospital and the Nashua Street Jail, the large building across Nashua Street from the Nashua Street Park. The park itself, however, is partly on land made by filling along the river from the 1930s through the 1960s by the state Department of Public Works.

This is the end of the walk. Nearest T station—Science Park (Green Line).

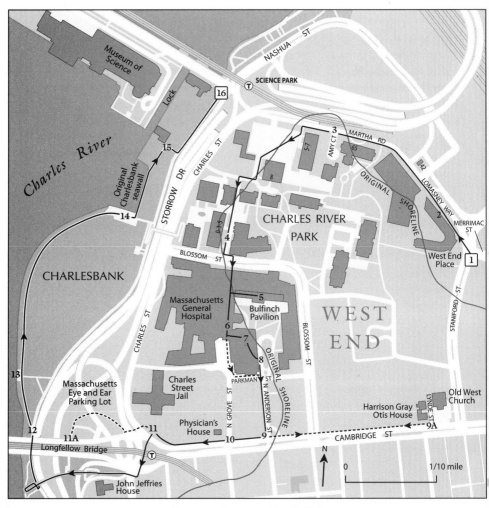

Current street map for Walk 3

Walk 3
WEST END AND CHARLESBANK

Distance: 2 ³/₅ miles (including optional detours)
Time: 1 ¹/₂ hours
Public Restrooms: MGH
Note: This walk goes up and down several flights of stairs.

This walk traces the landmaking in the West End, the section of Boston with Massachusetts General Hospital and the Charles River Park apartments whose "If you lived here . . . you'd be home now" signs are so familiar on Storrow Drive. It also covers the landmaking that created Charlesbank park, across Charles Street and Storrow Drive from the West End. As you can see from the *key map*, filling the West End involved filling the West Cove. On the walk you will follow the original shoreline of the West End, visit a historic building at Mass General, see other historic buildings in the West End, and trace the evolution of Charlesbank park.

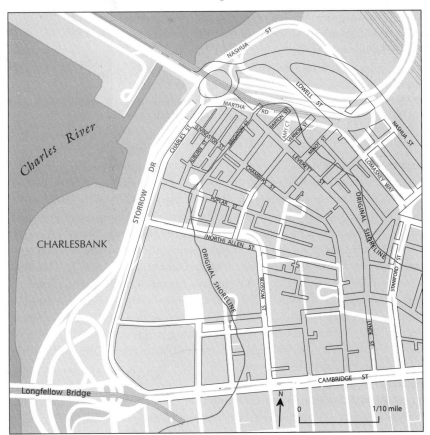

Pre-1958 streets on current street map

1   **Start at the corner of Staniford and Merrimac Streets.**

Nearest T station—North Station (Green/Orange Lines).

"West End" denotes not only a geographic area of Boston but is also the term applied to the neighborhood of densely packed tenements that once occupied the land where Charles River Park is now. In the late 1950s the West End neighborhood was demolished in an urban renewal project about which there is still much bitterness and replaced with the high rises of Charles River Park. Because this urban renewal project also obliterated the old streets in the West End neighborhood, the *pre-1958 street pattern* has been *overlaid on the current street map* to help you locate landmaking projects in relation to today's landmarks. Note West End Place (1997) at 150 Staniford Street, where West End residents displaced by the 1950s urban renewal project were supposed to get preferential housing.

2   **Start up Lomasney Way (the street on the right-hand side of West End Place).**

Lomasney Way was formerly Lowell Street, the northeastern boundary of the West End (*see overlay map*). It is on land made in 1835 for the depots of the Boston & Lowell Railroad (see Walk 2, ◆ p. 42, and *current street map*). As you start up the street, to your left is the original shoreline and the site of the 1820s jails and courthouse on Leverett Street (see p. 51 and *1826 and overlay maps*). Note the good view to the right of the Zakim Bridge. The building at 42 Lomasney Way (*photo*) is the last surviving tenement of the West End neighborhood.

42 Lomasney Way

3   **Continue up Lomasney Way/Martha Road to Amy Court.**

ALMSHOUSE

◆   The first landmaking project in the West End took place in 1799–1800 to create land for a new almshouse, a town-run institution to house the poor. In the 1700s, Boston's almshouse was at the corner of what are now Park and Beacon Streets across from the Common and the site of the State House. By 1790 this almshouse had become hopelessly inadequate—there were no separate quarters for the sick and the air in the courtyard was "noxious" because so many privies were jammed into the small space—so the town decided to build a new one. They eventually chose a site at the tip of the West End (*see 1800 map*), which at the time was a sparsely settled outlying district of Boston. The site was probably selected because it was far from the center of town—reflecting an "out-of-sight-out-of-mind" attitude toward public institutions—and because the land was cheap, since much of it was tidal flats that needed to be filled. In 1799 the town built a stone seawall around the perimeter of the almshouse site and then dumped fill (in this case probably mud from nearby flats) behind it until the level of fill was above the level of high tide—the customary method of making land in the 1800s. A brick almshouse

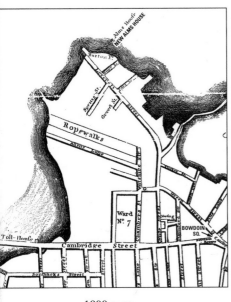

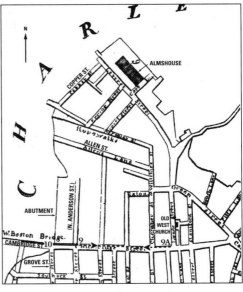

1800 map   1803 map

designed by architect Charles Bulfinch was then erected on the made land and opened in 1800 (*see 1803 map*). The almshouse site was in the Martha Road/Amy Court area—almost all of the Amy Lowell Apartments at 65 Martha Road, for example, is on land made for the almshouse (*see current street and overlay maps*).

Go around the end of 5–7 Whittier Place (the building on the far side   4
of Amy Court), cut diagonally through the parking lot, leave 8 Whittier
Place (the tall building) on your left and go straight through the brick-
paved open area. Turn right on the walk before the middle set of town
houses and then left on the walk between these town houses and the
town houses to the west, heading toward the 0–1–5 Emerson Place (yellow) building.

This route has taken you approximately along the 1630 shoreline of the West End (*see current street map*). The 0–1–5 Emerson Place building is on the site of a 1700s copper works—one of the industries located in the West End when it was an outlying district. Most of the land between the original shoreline, marked by Copper (later Brighton) Street (*see overlay map*), and Charles Street was made in the 1830s and 1840s when the West End needed more residential land (*see 1826 and 1852 maps*).

Cross Blossom Street and enter the Gray/Bigelow Building of Massa-   5
chusetts General Hospital (MGH). Go down the corridor labeled "Main,"
take the first left, and enter the Bulfinch Pavilion. Go down the corridor
to the display of historical photos titled "A Photographic Album."

MASSACHUSETTS GENERAL
HOSPITAL

In 1817 the trustees of the
Massachusetts General Hospital
(MGH), which had been chartered in 1811, decided to locate
the hospital on North Allen
(now Blossom) Street in the
West End. No landmaking was
necessary for the first building,
designed by Bulfinch and built
between 1818 and 1821 (*see current street map*). This building
became known as the Bulfinch
Pavilion and is the building you
are now in. The site chosen for
the Bulfinch Pavilion, however,

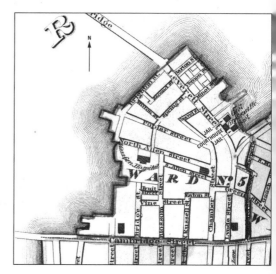

1826 map

meant discontinuing Bridge (now North Anderson) Street, which had been
extended to North Allen Street just a few years before. Instead, Blossom Street
was extended to North Allen and, as part of the agreement, required to remain
"forever open"—as it still is (*see 1826 and current street maps*). Look at the display
of historical photos for some further history of the hospital and this building.

To see the historic Ether Dome, take the optional detour below.
Otherwise, skip ahead to 6.

5A   Optional detour to the Ether Dome. Either go up the beautiful granite
      stairs or take the elevator (from the end of the historical photos go left,
      then right toward "Edwards Research") to the fourth floor.
      Go into the Ether Dome (open daily 9 AM–8 PM, with 1–3 PM reserved for vis-
      itors. If the door is locked, call Security on the house phone to be buzzed
      in)—the place where the first operation using ether anesthesia was per-
      formed—and read the plaque about its significance.

5   Return to the first floor.

6   From the Bulfinch Pavilion, retrace your
      route to the corridor to "Main," turn left, and
      continue down the corridor.
      Through the windows on the left you can see the
      Bulfinch Pavilion (*photo*) and, before the main
      entrance, a seawall in a pit. The seawall was dis-
      covered in the 1930s when the White Building

Bulfinch Pavilion

(the building you're now in) was being constructed. According to the MGH
historical plaque on the wall, the seawall was a wharf to which patients were
brought by boat. MGH *was* right on the Charles River until about 1870 but

1852 map

the date and function of the seawall are unclear. The seawall is parallel to the end of the Bulfinch Pavilion, as you can see, but an *1852 map* shows a curved shoreline at the end of the pavilion. Furthermore, an *1853 photo* of MGH shows tidal flats extending from the building to the river with no seawall in evidence

1853 photo of Bulfinch Pavilion and Harvard Medical School

at all. The flats between the Bulfinch Pavilion and Charles Street were filled in the 1860s (see below). The seawall for that project was built on the west (far) side of Charles Street, so it is not clear when or why the seawall next to the White Building was constructed.

7   **Just before the main entrance, turn left and go down the stairs to the Wang Lobby.**
Through the windows at the end of the lounge there is a good view of the Bulfinch Pavilion, especially when the leaves are off the trees.

8   **Exit to North Anderson (formerly Bridge) Street. (On weekends the exit from the Wang Lobby is closed. Instead, go back upstairs, go out the main MGH entrance, turn left on Parkman Street, and left on North Anderson.)**
Here is another good view of the Bulfinch Pavilion when the leaves are off the trees. You can also go and take a closer look at the seawall in the pit.

9   **Go down North Anderson Street to Cambridge Street. If you want to see some early 1800s buildings in the West End, take the optional detour below. Otherwise, skip ahead to 10.**

9A   **Optional detour to see early 1800s development in the West End. Turn left on Cambridge Street and go up it to Lynde Street.**
In 1793 the second bridge connecting the Boston peninsula to the mainland was constructed. It ran from West Boston, as the West End was then known, to Cambridge on the site of today's Longfellow Bridge. The bridge increased traffic through the West End, especially on Cambridge Street, the street leading to the bridge, and brought new residents and more trade. Bowdoin Square, just up Cambridge Street from where you are now (*see 1800 map*), became a fashionable residential area and the two buildings on either side of
♦   Lynde Street are survivals from that era. The first Harrison Gray Otis House (on the left; see *photo* in Walk 2, p. 40) was designed by Bulfinch and built in 1796 for an important Boston lawyer, politician, and participant in many
♦   early nineteenth-century landmaking projects. Old West Church (on the right; see *photo* in Walk 2, p. 40) was designed by architect Asher Benjamin and constructed in 1806—you can see it on the *1803 map*.

9   **Return to the corner of Cambridge and North Anderson Streets.**

10   **From the corner of Cambridge and North Anderson Streets, go west on Cambridge Street to North Grove Street.**
North Grove Street marks the line of an abutment, or wood bulkhead, constructed in 1799 on the flats north of the West Boston Bridge (see optional detour, above). The flats between the abutment and the shore were then filled in, making new land (*see 1800 and 1803 maps*) on which Bridge, now North Anderson, Street was laid out. The house on the west corner of North Grove

Street is the Resident Physician's House, built in 1891 at the corner of Allen and Blossom Streets (*see 1852 map*), moved in 1949 south on Blossom Street, and in 1982 to its present location.

Continue down Cambridge Street. In the early 1800s wharves were built out in front of the 1799 abutment (*see 1803 and 1826 maps*). So, as you continue down Cambridge Street, think wharves to your right. **Stop at the Charles Street Jail.**

CHARLES STREET JAIL

In the early 1820s the city, which also comprises Suffolk County, built a new courthouse and city and county jails on Leverett Street in the West End (*see 1826 and overlay maps*). But the county jail immediately proved unsatisfactory, for its design made it impossible to heat the cells in winter. In the 1830s and 1840s the city tried to decide whether to remodel or replace the jail and,

Charles Street Jail

if the latter, where to locate it. Finally, in 1848 the city chose a site for a new jail at the corner of Cambridge and North Grove Streets and purchased the requisite land and flats, much of them from Dr. George Parkman. Ironically, the next year Parkman was murdered, probably by Dr. John Webster, who was angry about the way Parkman had been hounding him to repay a debt. The murder was committed in the Harvard Medical School building, shown across from the Bulfinch Pavilion on the *1852 map and 1853 photo,* and was a great scandal at the time.

In late 1848 the city began building a seawall on the north and west sides of the jail site and filling the enclosed flats (*see 1826 and 1852 maps*). The new jail, a granite cruciform building designed by architect Gridley J. F. Bryant (*photo*), was then constructed on the made land and opened in 1851 (*see 1852 map*). The new county jail soon became known as the Charles Street Jail and served for well over a hundred years, finally being replaced in 1990 by the Nashua Street Jail (see Walk 2, ◆ p. 43). The north arm of the building (on the opposite side from where you are) was lengthened in 1901, the west arm (to the left) in 1920 (you can see the differences in the granites), and the east arm (on the right) demolished in 2001 to provide space for a new MGH building and then partly reconstructed in 2003. In an ironic twist, the remaining part of the jail is being converted into an upscale hotel.

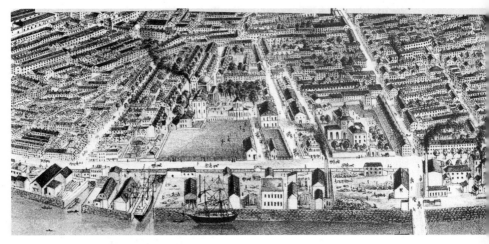

1870 bird's-eye view of MGH flats

MGH FLATS

After the land had been made for the Charles Street Jail, Charles Street was extended from the foot of Beacon Hill across this new land. Another piece of Charles Street had been laid out on the area filled west of Brighton Street in the 1840s (see p. 47 and *1852 map*) and the city wanted to connect the two sections of the street. The city originally planned to build a seawall and fill in the intervening flats, but MGH, which owned the flats, objected, so in 1858 the city built a bridge across the flats instead. But no sooner was the bridge finished than MGH decided it wanted to fill its flats after all, probably because the bridge, which was on closely spaced pilings, prevented the flats from being flushed out by the tide and they had become polluted. (For most of the 1800s sewers emptied at the nearest shoreline from where the sewage was supposed to be carried away by the outgoing tide.) So, in late 1859 the city contracted to have a seawall built across the MGH flats and the flats filled. By 1863 the new section of Charles Street was completed enough so that the city took down the bridge it had built just five years before. Filling the MGH flats continued during most of the 1860s and was apparently finished by *1870* when a *bird's-eye view* of that year shows the flats completely filled. In the bird's-eye you can see the recently completed Charles Street in the foreground crossing between Poplar Street at the left and Cambridge Street at the right (*see 1852 map*), the Charles Street Jail at the right, and the Bulfinch Pavilion (with a dome) behind the newly made land with the Harvard Medical School building across from it. Spanning the front of the view is the new seawall with two docks (slips) for ships.

To compare an 1892 photo of Charlesbank park with the present view, take the optional detour below. Otherwise, skip ahead to 12.

1892 photo of south end of Charlesbank

Optional detour. Cross the intersection toward the Longfellow Bridge 11A (be careful) as far as the entrance/exit gates of the Massachusetts Eye and Ear Infirmary parking lot, enter the lot, bear left under the viaduct, and go up the stairs to the Longfellow Bridge.

Compare the view at the top with that in the *1892 photo of Charlesbank* (best done when the leaves are off the trees), which was taken from the West Boston Bridge, the predecessor of the Longfellow Bridge. The road at the right-hand edge of the photo is Charles Street, so note that what was once the park is now the Massachusetts Eye and Ear Infirmary parking lot.

Retrace your route.

From Cambridge Street cross the traffic circle heading toward the four- 12 story brick building with segmental-arched windows and light stone trim (the John Jeffries House) on the far side. From in front of that building go up the stairs labeled "↑ Community Boating, Hatch Shell" to the pedestrian overpass over Storrow Drive. Near the end of the overpass note the nice view of the Longfellow Bridge, completed in 1907 on the site of the West Boston Bridge (see optional detour 11A above). **At the bottom of the stairs, turn left and go under the Longfellow Bridge to Charlesbank park.**

CHARLESBANK

The seawall built across the MGH flats in 1860 (see p. 52) was not destined to exist very long, for in the 1880s it was buried by the fill for a park. The new park—Charlesbank—was one of a system of public parks that Boston inaugurated in the 1870s. The park commissioners tried to place a park in each section of the city; Charlesbank was intended to serve the working-class residents of the West End tenements who, at least after the mid-1880s, were predominantly Eastern European Jews. Charlesbank was originally a narrow park along the river west of Charles Street. To construct it, a new seawall was built in 1885–1886 outside the 1860 wall, and the intervening space was then filled with material dredged from the river, covering the earlier wall (*see 1892 plan of Charlesbank*). Charlesbank was designed by Frederick Law Olmsted, the well-known landscape architect and the designer of all the original parks in the Boston system. Olmsted's design for Charlesbank had exercise areas for women and children at the south end near what is now the Longfellow Bridge (*see 1892 photo of Charlesbank*), a raised landscaped berm (mound) in the middle to shield the park from the rest of the city, and a large outdoor gymnasium for men and boys at the north end (*see 1892 plan of Charlesbank and 1910 photo* on p. 57).

Charlesbank was enlarged several times. In the early 1930s, when the Esplanade south of the Longfellow Bridge was widened, so was Charles Street and, to compensate for the land taken from the park, 5.8 acres of fill were added to the southern half of Charlesbank (*see 1931 plan*). At this time the Olmsted design was all but obliterated, for baseball diamonds and a track replaced the women and children's areas and a swimming pool was planned—though never built—in the outdoor gymnasium area. Charlesbank was widened again in 1950–1951 to compensate for land taken for Storrow Drive—the knot of ramps that entwine the Massachusetts Eye and Ear Infirmary parking lot are on land that was once part of the park (see optional detour 11A, p. 53). This time, 5.1 acres of fill were added, again to the southern part of the park (*see 1949 plan*).

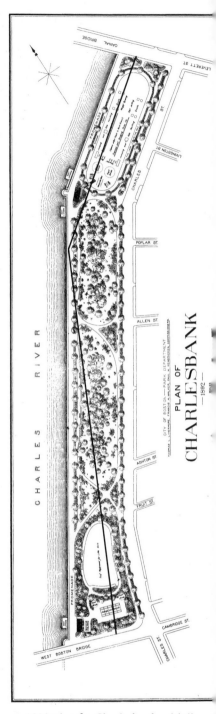

1892 plan for Charlesbank with line o 1860 seawall

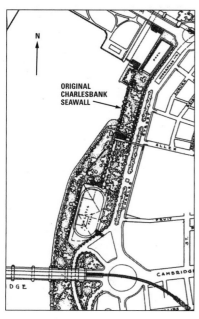

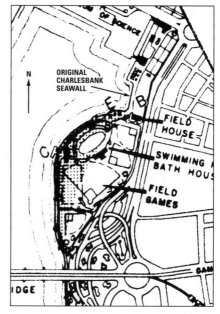

| 1931 plan | 1949 plan |

Take the walk along the shore of Charlesbank. 13

This walk is on the land made in 1950–1951. From the green-railed observation platform at the river's edge, note the stone riprap edging the 1950s fill (best seen in the winter when the weeds covering it are dead). The stones came from part of an 1850s and 1860s seawall south of the Longfellow Bridge (see Walk 4, ♦ p. 62) that was demolished in 1950 for the construction of the inbound tunnel of Storrow Drive. As you continue along the walk, note that the buildings between the Charles Street Jail and 0–1–5 Emerson Place (the yellow building in Charles River Park) are on land made by filling the MGH flats in the 1860s and so is the section of Charles Street that runs in front of them. Note also the good view of the Museum of Science on the first Charles River Dam (see p. 56).

Continue to the railing by the parking lot. 14

From the green railing at the river's edge by the parking lot there is a good view of the one remaining portion of the original Charlesbank seawall (*see current street, 1931, and 1949 maps*).

FIRST CHARLES RIVER DAM ♦

At the end of the 1800s Bostonians became concerned about the condition of the Charles River—after years of being at the receiving end of sewers discharging raw sewage, the flats in the river stank and looked revolting at low tide. In the 1890s several commissions considered the problem, finally recommending that a dam be built to maintain the water in the Charles River

1913 photo of Charles River Dam

Basin at a constant level that would keep the flats always covered with water—an out-of-sight, out-of-smell solution. The dam would also transform the salt water basin into a fresh water park modeled on the Alster Basin in Hamburg, Germany—a plan that had been proposed for years.

The dam was finally approved in 1903 and constructed on the site of Craigie's Bridge (*see 1852 map*) between 1905 and 1910. The project included a lock through the dam—you can get a good view of the lock from the railing by the parking lot. The project also included an **L**-shaped park on the upriver side of the dam. For years the park remained open (*see 1913 photo*), but in 1950 the Museum of Science erected a temporary building there, followed in 1951 by its first permanent building, and has since expanded to its present complex of buildings.

15 **Go along the river (next to the Charlesbank seawall) past the tot lot on the right to the junction of this walk and the one around the tennis courts.**

Note that the building on your left is the same one-story building, originally the upper lock gatehouse, shown next to the lock in *1913 and 1910 photographs* of the dam. And the building ahead of you with a tower, from which the *1910 photo* was taken—originally the lower lock gatehouse and bridge tender's tower—is also still standing (*see 1913 photo*). The tennis courts and part of Storrow Drive are on the site of the men and boys' gymnasium at Charlesbank (*see 1910 photo*).

1910 photo of Charles River Dam and Charlesbank

Jog right and then left around the tennis courts and continue to the   **16**
intersection of the Storrow Drive on-ramp and the highway across the
dam (the building with the tower will be on your left).
Note the 1910 viaduct, built on the dam to carry the elevated railway (now
the T) to Lechmere (*see 1913 photo*).

This is the end of the walk. Nearest T station—Science Park (Green Line).

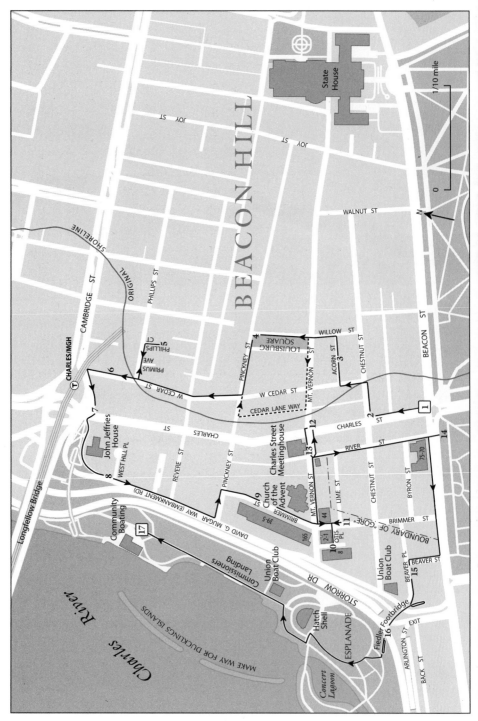

Current street map for Walk 4

Walk 4

BEACON HILL FLAT AND ESPLANADE

Distance: 2 miles
Time: 1 ¹/₄ hours
Note: This walk goes up a relatively steep hill.

This walk traces the land made at the foot of Beacon Hill by filling in flats along the Charles River, which was once a tidal estuary (*see key map*). On the Beacon Hill part of the walk you will see historic sites, such as Louisburg Square, cobble-stoned Acorn Street, and the Charles Street Meetinghouse. The walk also traces landmaking on the Esplanade in front of Beacon Hill where the Hatch Shell is located.

Start at the corner of Charles and Beacon Streets.   1
Nearest T stop—about equidistant from Park Street (Green/Red Lines), Arlington (Green Line), Boylston (Green Line), and Charles/MGH (Red Line).

MOUNT VERNON PROPRIETORS
In 1794 a group called the Mount Vernon Proprietors was formed to develop a residential area on the south slope of Beacon Hill—a type of development Boston needed at a time when its population was growing rapidly (see Walk 1, ♦ p. 13). The proprietors purchased the land now bounded by Beacon, Walnut, Mt. Vernon, Joy, and Pinckney Streets and what was then the river (*see current street map*). One of the proprietors, Harrison Gray Otis, was a member of the state committee selecting a site for the new State House, which they soon located on Beacon Street just a few blocks from the proprietors' property (*see current street map*), and it has been said that Otis used his inside information about the proposed site of the State House to buy up land for his residential venture while it was still cheap. But the committee to select a site for the new State House was not appointed until February 1795 and the Mount Vernon Proprietors were organized in 1794, so the case is not as clear-cut as is usually presented.

The Mount Vernon Proprietors' land encompassed the westernmost peak of Beacon Hill (for the location of the other two peaks, see Walk 2, ♦ pp. 37 and 38), whose summit was between present Mt. Vernon and Pinckney Streets a little east of Louisburg Square (*see current street map*). In the late 1700s this peak was known as "Mount Whoredom" because of a red light district on its north slope, but the proprietors changed the name to Mount Vernon as one more suitable for a residential area. The proprietors' plan was to grade   ♦
down Mount Vernon for house lots, dumping the resulting dirt on the flats   ♦
at the foot of the hill to make a new street. The new street—today's Charles   ♦
Street—is marked on an *1803 map* as "A street proposed to the Bridge." The
project got underway in 1803 and problems soon arose because the fill   ♦

dumped on the flats was washing away. So a wood abutment, or bulkhead, was built extending from Beacon to beyond Pinckney Street, probably on the line of River Street (*see current street map*).

2 **Go north on Charles Street to Chestnut Street.**

1803 map

Charles Street is on land made by the Mount Vernon Proprietors project. The original shoreline was to your right; Mount Vernon sloped down sharply toward both Beacon Street and the river, ending at a steep bank above the latter (*see current street map*). The corner of Charles and Chestnut marks the lower terminus of the most famous innovation on this project—an incline railway to haul fill (*see 1803 map*). The railroad operated on moveable wooden tracks with two sets of cars attached to each other through a large pulley at the top, so as one set of cars came down it pulled the other set up. This railroad was long reputed to be the first in the United States and a recent study concluded that it probably was.

3 **Go right on Chestnut Street, left on West Cedar Street,** noting that the original shoreline ran approximately through the present intersection of Chestnut and West Cedar Streets and then veered off toward present Charles Street (*see current street map*), **and right on Acorn Street.**

You are traversing the part of Beacon Hill that was developed by the Mount Vernon Proprietors, though many of the houses were not built until the 1830s and 1840s. Beacon Hill became a fashionable residential area in the 1820s and has remained so, populated then as now by many Boston "Brahmins." The houses on Acorn Street, noted for its charming cobblestones and gas street lamps, were built in the 1820s, perhaps for tradesmen or for coachmen at the large houses on Chestnut and Mt. Vernon Streets.

4 **At the top of Acorn Street, turn left on Willow Street to Louisburg Square and continue straight to Pinckney Street.**

Louisburg Square, which was laid out by the Mount Vernon Proprietors although most of the houses were not built until the 1830s and 1840s, epitomizes Beacon Hill elegance. The upper terminus of the early railroad that hauled fill down the hill was at the corner of the square and Pinckney Street (*see 1803 map*).

5 **Go left on Pinckney Street, right on West Cedar, and right on Phillips Street to Phillips Court (the first alley-like opening on the right after**

Primus Avenue). OR, if you want to see another very narrow street on Beacon Hill, from Louisburg Square go back to Mt. Vernon Street and turn right, turn right on Cedar Lane Way, right on Pinckney Street, left onto West Cedar Street, and then continue as above to Phillips Court. North of Phillips Street the 1630 shoreline curved inward, forming the south shore of the West Cove, most of which was in the West End (*see key map*). The walls you see in Phillips Court are thus not stone seawalls along the former shore, as some people think—the shoreline was of course on the *other* side of Phillips Street (*see current street map*)—but rather retaining walls to support houses on the cul-de-sacs off Revere Street because the hill descended so steeply here.

Phillips Street is on what is called the north slope of Beacon Hill. The north slope was developed in the 1700s, well before the south slope. A street grid was laid out and various neighborhoods developed—not only the red light district, which was at the west end of today's Phillips Street, but also, after Massachusetts abolished slavery in 1783, Boston's African-American community in the vicinity of what is now Joy Street. In the late 1800s and the first half of the 1900s, the north slope was populated by the same immigrant groups that lived in the West End on the other side of Cambridge Street—first Eastern European Jews and then Italians. In fact, further east on Phillips Street is the Vilna Shul, built in 1919 by a Jewish congregation of immigrants from Vilna, Lithuania. The north slope has always been considered less fashionable than the south slope, though now, with increased real estate values, the distinction is less clear than it once was.

Return down Phillips Street and turn right on West Cedar Street.

The section of Charles Street north of Pinckney Street—to your left as you go down West Cedar Street (*see current street map*)—was filled in 1805 by architect Charles Bulfinch, an original Mount Vernon Proprietor until he sold his shares in 1797. Bulfinch had bought these flats just after the West Boston (now

1807 map

Longfellow) Bridge opened in 1793. While the Mount Vernon Proprietors were filling their flats, Bulfinch continued their wood abutment (bulkhead) across his flats and, with the proprietors' permission, had his flats filled with earth from the north part of their land. Charles Street was probably bent between Mt. Vernon and Pinckney Streets to reduce the amount of filling necessary near the bridge, for had the street been continued in a straight line as shown on an *1807 map*, there would have been a much larger area to fill.

7   **Go to Cambridge Street and bear left to Charles Street.**

As you go from the end of West Cedar Street to Charles Street, note that the end of Cambridge Street to your right was filled in 1807 by the proprietors of the West Boston, or Cambridge, Bridge. Comparing the 1630 shoreline on the *current street map* with the shoreline shown on an *1814 map* shows that the land made in the first decade of the 1800s by the Mount Vernon Proprietors and others extended to about the line of present River Street.

8   **Go left on David G. Mugar Way (former Embankment Road) in front of the John Jeffries House.**

♦   1850s and 1860s Seawall

The east side of former Embankment Road is on the line of a seawall that was built across the Beacon Hill flats between the late 1840s and

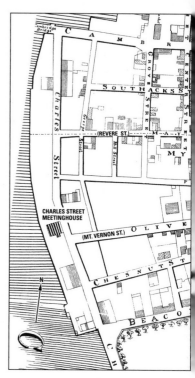

1814 map

the late 1860s. An 1850 state act ordered all the owners of shoreline property between what are now the Long-fellow Bridge and Back Street to build a wall on the harbor commissioners line—the line that limited how far out fill and wharves could extend. The shoreline owners were slow to comply. By 1852 the wall only reached just south of Southack Street (now West Hill Place; *see 1852 map*), by 1857 only to May (now Revere) Street, and by 1860 just to Pinckney Street. Note, by the way, on the *1852 map* that in the

1852 map

1830s and 1840s some of the made land west of Charles Street was being used commercially—there were various wharves, a marble yard, and a mahogany chair manufactory—and, behind the completed part of the seawall, a window sash factory and the 1849 building of the Massachusetts Eye and Ear Infirmary. Meanwhile, concern had grown about the flats at the foot of Mt. Vernon Street, which had become polluted by a sewer outlet there. (For most of the 1800s, raw sewage was discharged at the nearest shoreline from where it was supposed to be flushed away by the outgoing tide.) The city decided the solution was to finish the seawall across the Beacon Hill flats and extend the sewer out beyond it. So in 1860 the state legislature passed another act depriving shoreline owners of all rights to their flats unless they built their sections of the wall in two years. An *1866 bird's-eye view* shows the new seawall extending across the flats and filling going on behind it. Note how far inland the Charles Street Meetinghouse is in this view in comparison with its position on the water on the *1852 map*.

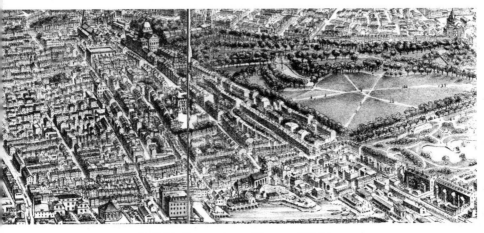

1866 bird's-eye view of Beacon Hill Flat

At Pinckney Street, turn left and then turn right on Brimmer Street.　　9

FALLING GROUNDWATER/ROTTING FOUNDATION PILES　　◆

You are on land made in the 1860s when the flats behind the seawall next to Embankment Road were filled. This area has been particularly subject to falling groundwater and rotting foundation piles—one of the serious problems that has occurred in some filled areas of Boston. Most of the brick or stone buildings constructed in the 1800s on made land in Boston are supported by wood pilings driven through the fill to the underlying clay or other glacial deposits as shown in the *diagram of falling groundwater/rotting foundation piles*. When these pilings were driven in the 1800s, their tops were cut off well below the normal level of groundwater (*see diagram*) because wood is preserved almost indefinitely if always submerged in water. In the 1900s, however, the groundwater level began dropping in many parts of Boston, mainly because of leaks into sewers (the elliptical opening in the *diagram*), "T" tunnels, and other subsurface structures. As a result, the tops of the pilings supporting building foundations were exposed to air and, since when wet wood is exposed to air it is subject to bacteria that cause rot, many pilings began rotting, leaving the foundations above them unsupported and causing serious structural damage to the buildings (*see* inset enlargment in lower right-hand corner of *diagram*). The problem can be fixed by underpinning, an expensive process that involves excavating by hand beneath damaged buildings, cutting off the rotted portion of the pilings, and replacing them with steel pilings encased in concrete.

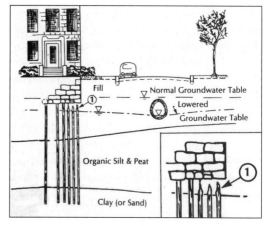

Diagram of falling groundwater/
rotting foundation piles

In 1984 large cracks began to appear in houses you are passing on the water (west) side of Brimmer Street between Pinckney and Mt. Vernon Streets. The cause was rotted foundation pilings, and eventually all nineteen houses on this side of the street had to be underpinned at a cost of $130,000 to $300,000 per house. In this case, the lowered groundwater was caused by leaks into the sewers on Pinckney and Mt. Vernon Streets.

The Church of the Advent, at the corner of Brimmer and Mt. Vernon Streets, has not been underpinned but monitors the groundwater level carefully, pumping in water if necessary to keep its foundation pilings submerged.

10 **Cross Mt. Vernon Street and turn right into Otis Place.**
The house at 8 Otis Place dropped several inches with a loud rumbling and shaking one night in 1986—a victim of rotted foundation piles. Note that this house backs onto the seawall next to Embankment Road, is in the area filled in the 1860s, and is also near Mt. Vernon Street—so it was probably leaks into that sewer that caused the lowered groundwater and consequent rotted pilings.

11 **Return to Brimmer Street,** noting the house at no. 44 on the other side of the street, which was the home of historian Samuel Eliot Morison and featured in his autobiography, *One Boy's Boston,* and cross Brimmer Street to **the southeast corner of Brimmer and Lime Streets.**

1870 photo of 1–2 Otis Place

Compare the present view of the double house at 1–2 Otis Place with that in a c. *1870 photo*, noting how close this house was to the river before the Esplanade was filled (see p. 67).

Charles Street Meetinghouse

Return on Brimmer Street to Mt. Vernon Street, turn right, and go to Charles Street. 12

Note the bend in Charles Street to the north (see p. 61 for an explanation of this bend). Also note the Charles Street Meetinghouse (*photo*), designed by architect Asher Benjamin and built in 1807 on land made by the Mt. Vernon Proprietors (*see 1814 map*).

From Charles Street, return down the north side of Mt. Vernon Street to River Street. 13

The multicolored house at the corner of Mt. Vernon and River Streets, which is known as the "Sunflower House" for the carving under the gable on the Mt. Vernon Street side, was built in 1840 and then transformed into this Queen Anne–style cottage in 1878.

Turn left on River Street, noting that the land on the left was made by the Mount Vernon Proprietors in 1803–1805 and, after Lime Street, the land on the right was added in the 1820s as part of the "gore" project, which is explained on p. 66 (*see 1814, 1826, and current street maps*). **Go down to Beacon Street and cross to the other side.** 14

THE "GORE"

In 1821 the town gave the Mount Vernon Proprietors permission to fill a "gore" (a triangular piece of land) of flats adjoining the Mill Dam, the dam built across the entire Back Bay in 1821 on the line of Beacon Street (see Walk 6, ◆ p. 89). The gore included flats just west of today's River Street that for years townspeople had used as a trash dump, so these flats were already partially filled. The proprietors built a stone seawall and wood abutment on the west line of the intended gore and filled the rest of the enclosed flats with
◆ dirt. The gore, which was actually a trapezoid rather than a triangle (*see 1826 map*), included present Byron and Lime Streets and parts of Brimmer and Chestnut Streets (*see current street map*). The houses still standing across the street from you at 70–75 Beacon Street (*photo*) were built in 1828 on the newly filled gore.

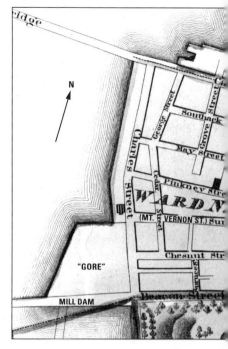

1826 map

15 **Cross back across Beacon Street, turn left, turn right on Beaver Street (the next street after Brimmer), and turn left on Beaver Place.**

Beaver Place is on land made in the 1860s after the seawall was built on the line of David G. Mugar Way (Embankment Road; *see current street map*). The stables and carriages houses on the street are typical of the original

70–75 Beacon Street

use of land on the Beacon Hill Flat, which was known as the "horsey end of town." Beaver Place is just south of the site of Braman's Baths—a public swimming and bathing establishment founded in 1835 by Jarvis Braman at the foot of Chestnut Street next to the gore. You can see Braman's Baths on both the *1852 map* and the *1866 bird's-eye view*. On the latter, the baths are behind the right-hand end of the seawall and the surrounding area is being filled.

Continue down Beaver Place and cross Storrow Drive on the Arthur
Fiedler Footbridge, stopping on the bridge over the curb on the far side
of the drive.

From the footbridge you have a good view (especially when the leaves are off the trees) of the Concert Lagoon, Hatch Shell, and "Make Way for Ducklings" islands (*see current street map*), features created by the various landmaking projects on the Esplanade that are explained below.

ESPLANADE

When the first Charles River Dam was built in 1905–1910 (see Walk 3, ♦ p. 55), converting the Charles River Basin from a tidal estuary to a body of fresh water that was supposed to become a "water park," the project also called for filling a narrow park along the Boston shore. Called the Boston Embankment, the section next to the Beacon Hill Flat was to be about three hundred feet wide. The embankment was created in 1906–1908 and Embankment Road (now David G. Mugar Way) was laid out on the new land next to the 1860s seawall, which had been covered over. The Union Boat Club then built a new boathouse on the made land (*see 1925 aerial photo*).

The water park did not work out as anticipated, however. Winds sweeping ♦ across the basin created waves that bounced off the seawalls, creating a chop that was dangerous for rowing shells and other small boats. In addition, the Back Bay section of the embankment was too narrow for boathouses. So in 1929, after years of protests, a commission recommended almost doubling the width of what by then was called the Esplanade, reducing the chop by sloping the shore down to the water's edge rather than ending it with a seawall, and adding some recreational facilities. In the section in front of the Beacon ♦ Hill Flat, the Esplanade was widened about 155 feet, covering the 1906–1908 seawall except at Commissioners Landing, one of the three neo-classical granite boat landings constructed on the Esplanade during the 1930s widening (the other two are at Dartmouth and Gloucester Streets—see Walk 6, ♦ p. 107). In contrast to the other two landings, which are at the outer edge of the 1930s fill, Commissioners Landing, which is just north of the Union Boat Club, is built on the line of the 1906–1908 seawall (*see 1934 aerial photo and current street map*). Opposite the landing two curved dikes were filled to create a haven for small boats—the "Make Way for Ducklings" islands (so-named because that is where Mr. and Mrs. Mallard of the eponymous book nested). At the time, the project's landscape architect noted that these islands could also serve as a place where crews of swamped shells could empty their boats "without shocking the people on shore because of their scanty attire." At the south end of the new land a concert shell was built with a "music lawn" in front of it (*see 1934 aerial photo*).

But one major planned change to the Esplanade in the 1930s was not con- ♦ structed—a highway along the river. It was dropped because of public opposition, particularly from Mrs. James J. Storrow, whose $1 million gift was

1925 aerial photo of the Boston Embankment in front of Beacon Hill

financing part of the recreational improvements. After World War II, however, the highway was deemed a necessary solution for Boston's "traffic mess" and, despite many protests, was rammed through the legislature and constructed in 1950–1951. It was ironically named Storrow Memorial Drive, in spite of Mrs. Storrow's earlier opposition, because it was on the Storrow Memorial Embankment, as the Esplanade had been named in the 1930s in honor of her gift. The drive was built on the part of the Esplanade filled in the first decade of the 1900s, and, to compensate for the land taken, more land was added. In the section next to the Beacon Hill Flat, an island was filled to create a "concert lagoon" (*see current street map*). And to preserve seating at the Hatch Shell, the inbound lane of Storrow Drive was put in a tunnel. Construction of the tunnel necessitated dismantling the section of the 1860s seawall between the Storrow Drive exit at Arlington Street (behind you) and the Union Boat Club building (the brick building to your right with a flag-

pole on top) at 144 Chestnut Street. The granite blocks from the wall were then used to edge the new fill added to Charlesbank (see Walk 3, ♦ p. 55).

17 From the end of the footbridge, turn right, go along the shore around the Hatch Shell (*photo*), and continue north.

Hatch Shell

1934 aerial photo of the Esplanade

Note the Concert Lagoon created by an island filled in 1950–1951, the concert lawn and Make Way for Ducklings islands filled in the 1930s, the Union Boat Club *(photo)* on land made in 1906–1908, and the 1906–1908 seawall under the balustrade at Commissioners' Landing *(photo;* best viewed from the wood piers in front of the Union Boat

Union Boat Club

Club or at the far end of Commissioners' Landing). Near the north end of the Esplanade note Community Boating, a public sailing facility on land made in

the 1930s, and the sailboat frieze on the Community Boating building erected in the 1940s.

This is the end of the walk. Nearest T station—Charles/MGH (Red Line)

1906–1908 seawall at
Commissioners' Landing

W
A
L
K

4

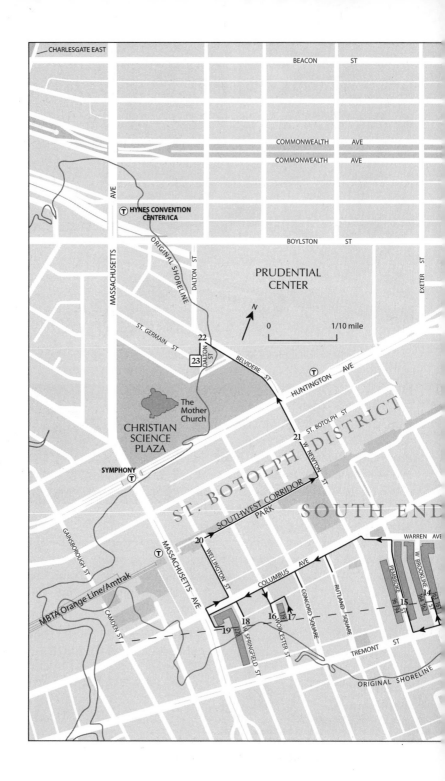

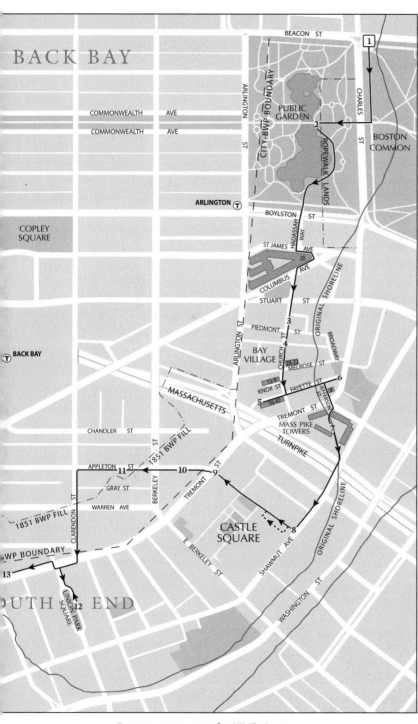

Current street map for Walk 5

Walk 5

PUBLIC GARDEN, BAY VILLAGE, SOUTH END, AND DALTON STREET AREA

Distance: 3 2/5 miles
Time: 2 1/4 hours

This walk traces landmaking around the edges of the original Back Bay, a large tidal bay on the *back* side of the Boston peninsula (*see map of made land*)—presumably the origin of its name. As you can see on the *current street map*, the original back bay of the Charles River extended as far south as today's Washington Street. It thus included, in addition to the area today generally regarded as Back Bay—that bounded by Beacon, Arlington, and Boylston Streets and Charlesgate East—the Public Garden and its Swan Boats, the charming Bay Village district with streets lined with 1830s row houses, Castle Square, some of the South End with its handsome nineteenth-century town houses and distinctive residential squares, Southwest Corridor Park, the St. Botolph District, the Christian Science Center, and the Dalton Street area. It is these latter areas that will be explored on this walk; landmaking in Back Bay proper is traced on Walk 6.

1   **Start at the corner of Beacon and Charles Streets.**
Nearest T stop—about equidistant from Park Street (Green/Red Lines), Arlington (Green Line), Boylston (Green Line), and Charles/MGH (Red Line). Enter the Common and, if you wish, read the "Charles Street" panel on the

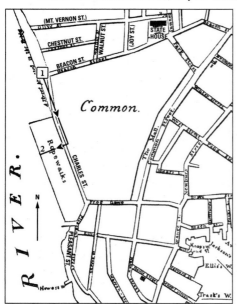

1803 map

historical kiosk. (Some of the information on this panel is at variance with information presented in Walk 2, ♦ p. 39, and Walk 4, ♦ p. 59.)

CHARLES STREET
The original shoreline was near the foot of the Common (*see current street map*) and by the end of the 1700s most of Charles Street along the Common had been laid out. The small triangle at the corner of Charles and Beacon Streets was filled by the town in 1803–1804 to connect the part of Charles Street next to the Common with the part of the street being filled by the Mount Vernon Proprietors (see Walk 4, ♦ p. 59, and *1803 map*).

Take the roadway in the Common parallel to Charles Street. At the
opening in the iron fence, cross Charles Street to the Public Garden and
go straight ahead to the bridge.

2

ROPEWALK LANDS

The first landmaking in Back Bay took place in 1794 and was the result of
disaster. In July 1794 the ropewalks on Fort Hill (site of present International
Place) burned. Ropewalks were very long narrow structures in which rope was
made by workers walking backward twisting hemp fibers into rope. When a
length of cordage was finished it was dipped into a vat of hot tar to waterproof it, and those vats of hot tar made ropewalks highly flammable structures. After the 1794 fire, the town moved quickly to relocate the ropewalks
away from habited areas, giving the proprietors (owners) of the ropewalks
some flats at the foot of the Common on condition they build a seawall, presumably so they would fill the intervening flats, which they did. The section
of the Public Garden you have been crossing is this land made for the ropewalks in 1794 (*see current street and 1803 maps*).

The ropewalks burned again in 1806 and also in 1819, so in 1822 the proprietors offered to *sell* back to the town the area the town *gave* them in 1794.
The city finally did buy the "ropewalk lands," as they were called, in 1824
but then was unwilling to assume the expense of building a seawall and filling the adjacent flats.

PUBLIC GARDEN

Finally, in 1830, because the flats west of Charles Street had become "offensive" from having been used as a trash dump since at least 1799, the city
decided to build a dike at the furthest extent of its flats and to fill them, sloping the shore down to the river. Most of the flats were apparently filled by
1837 when the city leased the area to Horace Gray and his associates to be
developed as a botanical garden, soon known as the Public Garden.

Go down the steps on the left just before the bridge and follow the walk
next to the water. Note that you are traversing the "ropewalk lands" (*see current street map*). Exit from the Public Garden halfway between Charles and
Arlington Streets, cross Boylston Street, go down Hadassah Way toward
the 20 Park Plaza building, go left and then right all the way around the
building, cross Columbus Avenue, go down Church Street (between
Maggiano's Little Italy restaurant and the park), cross Stuart Street, and
enter Bay Village.

3

BAY VILLAGE (CHURCH STREET DISTRICT)

You are now in Bay Village, an area formerly known as the Church Street
District after the street down its center. This district was originally bounded
by the Providence Railroad (now St. James Avenue), Arlington, Tremont, and
Pleasant (now Broadway) Streets but only the section south of Stuart Street
now remains (*see current street map*).

W
A
L
K

5

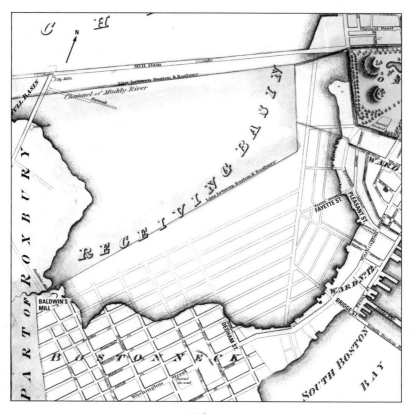

1826 map

Most of Bay Village is on land made in the 1820s and 1830s—only the part near Broadway, formerly Pleasant, is on original land (*see 1803 and current street maps*). In the mid-1820s the owners of flats west of Pleasant Street wanted the water of Back Bay cut off so they could fill their flats. The city, too, wanted to fill its flats on the shore of Back Bay, so in 1826 the city built a dike from Baldwin's Mill (now the intersection of Gainsborough Street and the Orange Line/Amtrak tracks—*see current street map and 1836 map* in Walk 7, p. 110) to Fayette Street in the Church Street District (*see 1826 map*). The shoreline owners then proceeded to fill their flats and by the mid-1830s the made land extended west of Church Street (*see 1835 map*). Many of the houses built in the 1830s in the Church Street District still exist—one of the charms of this neighborhood.

At the time the Church Street District was filled, the water in Back Bay was kept well below the level of high tide so that the mills in Back Bay could operate at all times (see p. 78). This meant that Bay Village did not have to be filled above the high tide yet the sewers serving the houses built on the fill could still drain at high tide. (For most of the 1800s, sewers discharged raw sewage at the nearest shoreline from where it was supposed to be carried off

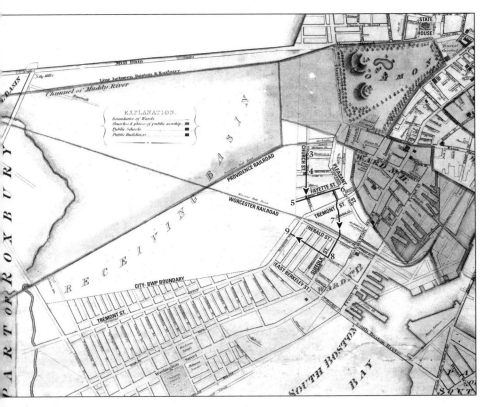

1835 map

by the ebb tide.) But when the part of Back Bay adjacent to the Church Street District was filled in the late 1850s and early 1860s, the sewers serving the district were rerouted to shorelines with normal tidal fluctuations. The result was that the sewers in the Church Street District could no longer drain at all at high tide and, when heavy rain storms occurred at high tide, the sewers, filled with storm water and sewage, backed up into people's cellars and other low-lying areas. In the 1860s the city considered several solutions: fill up the cellars and abandon them, install pumps to drain the sewers, or raise the ground level of the district by adding more fill. Surprising as it may seem today, the city

1868 photo of Church Street District

♦   chose the last alternative and in 1868 began raising the level of the Church Street District. Buildings were jacked up and underpinned (*see 1868 photo of Church Street District*), gravel fill brought in by railroad was placed under them, and then the buildings were returned to their owners. (This was a project that for once can correctly be termed landfilling rather than landmaking, since it was existing land that was filled.)

4   **Go down Church Street.**

28–22 Melrose Street

On Piedmont Street look left—the original shoreline was between Shawmut Street extension (the first street) and Broadway (the second street where there is a new building with a four-story green bay). At Melrose Street look left at the houses at 28–22 Melrose (*photo*), which do not appear to have been raised because their bottom floor windows are below street level and their front doors not much above the street. Historical records, however, indicate these houses were intended to be raised.

5   **Turn right on Fayette Street.**
The houses at 42–56 Fayette Street are reportedly those shown in the *1868 photo of the Church Street District,* so obviously were raised. Through the schoolyard fence on Fayette Street, look at the houses across the parking lot at 9–13 Knox Street (a half block north of Fayette), which were also raised.

6   **Retrace your route on Fayette Street, cross Church Street, and continue to the east end of Fayette Street.**
The brick walk on the west side of the park between Fayette and Melrose Streets is a continuation of Broadway, originally Pleasant Street, and thus on original land (*see 1803, 1826, and 1835 maps*).

7   **Retrace your route on Fayette, turn left on Jefferson Street** (note the original house at no. 9), **cross Tremont Street, and enter Mass Pike Towers through the gate in the iron fence.**

Suffolk Street District

♦   In 1829 the city decided to increase access to the land it owned south of the Neck (labeled "Boston Neck" on the *1826 map*, now part of the South End— *see current street map*) by filling some new streets to it. On the west side of the Neck, the major new street was Tremont, which the city constructed by building a mud dike, probably on the line that divided the city's flats from those of the Boston Water Power Company (*see 1835 and current street maps*), and then filling the intervening flats with mud. The city's dike also enabled the private owners of the flats between the Church Street District, which ended at Tremont Street, and the city's flats, which began at what is now East Berkeley Street, to fill their flats, creating what was called the Suffolk Street District after a street (now Shawmut Avenue) running through it (*see 1835 map*). What was once the Suffolk Street District is now the Mass Pike Towers and Castle Square housing areas (*see current street map*).

Like the Church Street District, the Suffolk Street District was not originally filled above the level of high tide because the water in Back Bay was kept abnormally low, and, like the Church Street District, when filling the major part of Back Bay began in the late 1850s and the sewers were rerouted, the Suffolk Street District began to flood with storm water and sewage during storms at high tide. And like the Church Street District, the city's solution was to raise the ground level of the entire district. The Suffolk Street District was raised between 1870 and 1872—again, one of the few instances in Boston of a landfilling rather than landmaking project.

♦

In Mass Pike Towers, bear left heading toward the Boston Herald building and leaving the tot lot on your right, and exit onto Shawmut Avenue (originally Suffolk Street). Cross the Mass Pike on Shawmut Avenue, continue down Shawmut past two streets to the first entrance on the right through the iron fence (opposite Holy Trinity German

8

1927 photo of Shawmut Avenue

Catholic Church) to the Castle Square development. Like Mass Pike Towers, Castle Square is on land that was once the Suffolk Street District, an area that, as explained above, was filled twice—once in the 1830s and again in the early 1870s. The appearance of the district just south of here is shown in a *1927 photo of Shawmut Avenue.* This part of the former Suffolk Street District south of the Mass Pike was demolished in 1964. Castle Square was then built on the cleared land in 1967 as a low- and moderate-income housing project, which it still is, though it is now tenant-controlled.

Enter Castle Square and go straight across, exiting under the building at the end onto Tremont Street opposite Appleton Street. OR, if you want to see more of Castle Square, jog left leaving the basketball court on your left, at the end of the court turn right and continue past buildings 15–23, and at the end of building 23 jog right and then left onto the walk first described.

9

10 Cross Tremont Street and go down Appleton Street.

BOSTON WATER POWER COMPANY FLATS

In 1818–1821 a dam was built across the entire Back Bay on the line of Beacon Street from Charles Street at the foot of the Common to today's Kenmore Square in order to power some tide mills. After 1832 the mills were operated by the Boston Water Power Company (BWP), which also had the right to keep the flats in Back Bay covered with water. The mills were never very successful, however, and in the 1840s the BWP determined that it would be more profitable to fill its flats and sell the made land for building lots. Thus, between 1846 and 1851 the BWP filled about eighteen acres west of Tremont Street—the land you are traversing on Appleton Street in the block from Tremont to Berkeley Street (*see current street map*).

11 Continue on Appleton Street past Berkeley.

BACK BAY PROJECT

As explained in Walk 6, ♦ p.91, by the mid-1800s Back Bay had become very polluted by the raw sewage draining into it from sewers serving the surrounding areas, and most agreed the solution was to fill Back Bay and develop the made land for residential use. The state and the BWP divided the flats south of the Mill Dam, the state getting about one hundred acres in part of the area now known as Back Bay and the BWP all the rest, including the area

♦ where you are now. The BWP began filling its flats in 1855, originally with dirt brought by horse-drawn tip carts. In 1858 the state contracted to have its flats filled with gravel, which was hauled from suburban Needham by railroad, and in 1859 the BWP made a similar contract, so most of the BWP's flats were also filled with gravel brought from Needham by rail. By 1861 the BWP had expanded the area north of Tremont Street that it had filled in 1846–1851 (*see current street and 1861 maps*—the long tongue of fill on Dartmouth Street may have been to support a railroad track).

Not all the BWP's filling met with approval. In 1863 residents on Appleton and Clarendon Streets sent the following letter to the president of the BWP:

Boston May 19, 1863

Dear Sir:

In view of the approaching warm weather and the season in which mosquitoes . . . most do congregate, we the residents and owners of buildings in Appleton and Clarendon Streets do respectfully but most earnestly call your attention to the condition of the lands (now unoccupied except by frogs, pollywogs and other insects) fronting on Appleton Street.

Possibly in the multiplicity of your duties it may not have occurred to you that the droves of mosquitoes which are generated in the stagnant water now covering this land constitute a nuisance. . . .

We view with alarm the already immense flocks of these nefarious insects about to fatten upon our wives and innocent babes—mercy is not one of their attributes—innocent childhood is bathed in blood—defenseless woman is made to feel the fangs of the tormentor—and our nights and much needed rest is utterly destroyed by this fearful visitation.

Are we then to submit patiently and endure these evils simply because the Boston Water Power Co. fail to perform their duty? Must our maidens and hand-maidens and wives and children be tortured and bled, perhaps carried off or eaten up without any redress? We think not! We believe not! We are assured that it cannot be! that common humanity will cry out against it, and we do most earnestly urge upon you to see to it at once, immediately and without delay, that this stagnant water is removed and these evils averted. . . .

Very Res'py Yours
(31 signatures)

It is not clear what action, if any, the BWP took in response, but it is clear that the south side of Appleton between Berkeley and Clarendon Streets, which you are passing, is the 1863 breeding ground of the nefarious mosquitoes.

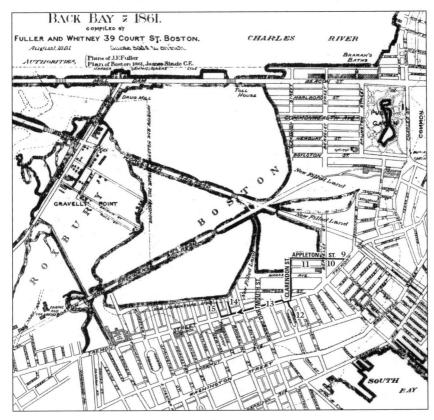

1861 map

W
A
L
K

5

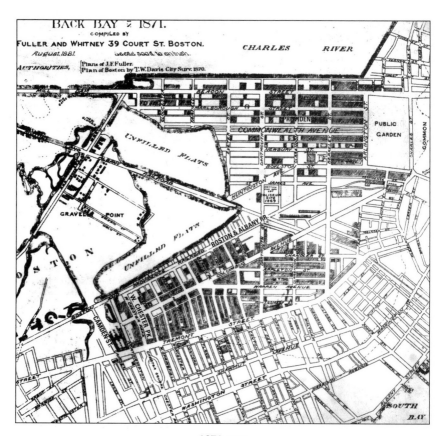

1871 map

By 1871 the BWP had finished filling the South End, whose northern boundaries were the railroad tracks that are now under Southwest Corridor Park and next to the Mass Pike (*see current street and 1871 maps*).

Appleton Street is in the Ellis Neighborhood section of the South End—so-named after the Ellis Memorial building at the corner of Berkeley and Chandler Streets, headquarters of a social service agency founded in 1885 and named for Reverand Rufus Ellis, minister of the First Church in Boston. When the Back Bay project began, it was originally intended that the streets in the South End part of the project be on the same grid as those in what is now called Back Bay. But bridges were built across the railroad tracks (see pp. 84–85) only on Arlington, Berkeley, Clarendon, and Dartmouth Streets (*see current street map*), so only the part of the South End between those streets—the Ellis Neighborhood—has the same street grid as Back Bay.

12   **At Clarendon Street, turn left and go down it, looking into Gray Street** (another charming street in the Ellis Neighborhood), **cross Tremont Street, turn right, and turn left into Union Park Square.**

You are in the South End section of Boston, so-called because it is south of Boston Neck—the narrow strip of land that connected the original Boston peninsula and the mainland (*see key map*). Part of the South End is original land (*see current street map*) and belonged to the town of Boston, which tried to develop it in the early 1800s. The town laid out a street grid, but even the filling of some new streets, such as Tremont Street (see p. 76), in the 1830s to provide more access routes besides Washington Street did not spur settlement. Development of the South End really began in the late 1840s when the city, wanting to encourage Yankees to remain in the city both as tax payers and as voters to counter the Irish, who were pouring into Boston at that time, decided to develop the South End as an upper-middle-class residential area. So, in the late 1840s, the city laid out streets, planted trees, built sewers, and in the early 1850s laid out the area's distinctive squares. Union Park Square, where you are now, if one of the nicest of these squares.

The city filled much of the South Bay side of the South End in 1845–1862 (see Walk 10, ♦ p. 153) and, as explained on p. 78, the BWP filled the remaining Back Bay side of the South End in the 1850s and 1860s. Elegant brownstone and brick row houses were then built in the South End, many with bow fronts and ornate cast iron stair railings. But the South End was considered a desirable residential area only through the 1860s. Cheaper housing along Columbus Avenue lowered the area's prestige, and in the financial panic of 1873 many houses were acquired by banks, which sold them at low prices. Many residents soon moved to the more fashionable Back Bay, and the South End then became a neighborhood of immigrants and rooming houses. It remained so until the 1960s, when middle-class residents began buying and renovating the once stately town houses. The trend has continued and the South End is now considered one of the city's choicest neighborhoods, replete with fine restaurants and trendy shops.

Return to and cross Tremont Street and turn left.   13

As you go down Tremont, remember that this area was filled in the 1830s (see p. 76) at the same time as the Church and Suffolk Street Districts, that is, when the water in Back Bay was kept well below the level of high tide, so surrounding areas did not need to be filled above high tide. Actually, in the case of the Tremont Street area, the streets were filled above high tide but the house lots were not. In fact, the latter were later described as low-lying areas enclosed by street embankments.

Turn right on West Brookline Street and go up to 162 and 164 on the   14
left and 161 and 163 on the right.

When the BWP began to fill its flats in the 1850s, however, it was required by the state to fill them above the level of high tide. This means that the parts of the South End filled by the city in the 1830s—on the south side of the line that marked the boundary between city and BWP flats (*see 1835 and current*

W
A
L
K

5

street maps)—are much lower than those filled by the BWP in the 1850s and 1860s. And there are places where you can actually see this difference. Look at 161 and 163 West Brookline on the right side of the street (*photo*) and 162 and 164 on the left (*photo*). In both cases the striking difference in height of the front doors and first floor windows is because the low house is on city-filled land and the high house is on BWP fill. If you look carefully, you can also see that the wall between 161 and 163 is not perpendicular to the facades of these houses because it is on the city–BWP boundary line, which ran diagonally through the South End (*see current street map*).

161 and 163
West Brookline Street

15 **Return to Tremont Street, turn right, turn right on Pembroke Street, and go up to 94 and 96 Pembroke on the left.**
The houses at 94 and 96 Pembroke (*photo*) are two other adjacent ones that are on different levels because they are on either side of the city–BWP line.

♦ The fact that the Tremont Street area was not filled above the high tide has caused serious problems for the residents of this section of the South End. Like the Church and Suffolk Street Districts, once the BWP filled its flats and the sewers were rerouted from Back Bay to South Bay, the Tremont Street area began to flood when storms occurred at high tide. But unlike the two other districts, the South End was not raised because it was not quite as low. The result was that for years during heavy rains that coincided

162 and 164
West Brookline Street

with high tide, storm water mixed with sewage backed up into houses in the Tremont Street area. Finally, in 1915 the city built a pumping station on Union Park Street (see Walk 10, ♦ p. 151) to pump up the effluent from the low-lying sewers, an alternative that was reasonable in 1915 when electrically powered pumps could be turned on with the flick of a switch but had not been

94 and 96 Pembroke Street

acceptable in the 1860s when pumps were steam powered, which would have necessitated their being manned and the boilers kept fired at all times.

For many years the Union Park Pumping Station seemed to have solved the flooding in the South End, but about 1980 residents in the Tremont Street area again began having sewage back up into their houses when heavy rains occurred at high tide. The city eventually hired an engineering firm to study the problem. The firm found multiple causes of the flooding, of which a major one was that the pumping station was not being operated properly. (Flooding occurred in a September 1999 storm, for example, because the fuel pumps to the turbines failed just at high tide.) But since 2000, when the pumping station has been under new management, there have been no floods in the South End and the problem seems to be under control.

Continue up Pembroke Street, turn left on Warren and then Columbus Avenues, look into Rutland and Concord Squares on the left—two more of the distinctive South End squares—**and turn left on Worcester Street.**

16

Note the bend in Worcester Street near Columbus Avenue, which will be explained on p. 85. The house on the left at 139 Worcester Street (*photo*) is an example, like the houses at 161 and 163 West Brookline Street, of a house whose lot line is the diagonal boundary between city and BWP flats. (Most of the lots abutting this boundary were squared off.) Look at

Front of 139 Worcester Street

the front of 139 Worcester, noting that it is two bays (main window or door openings reading across a building; the bay window occupies one bay) wide with an angled side wall next to the iron fence.

Retrace your route on Worcester Street, turn right into the alley between 149 and 153 Worcester, turn right into the alley behind the houses on Worcester Street, and go down to the iron fence next to 139 Worcester.

17

Note that, in contrast to the front, the back of the house at 139 Worcester (*photo*) is three bays wide—the result of its being on the diagonal city–BWP boundary line.

Back of 139 Worcester Street

18 **Return to Columbus Avenue, turn left, and turn left into West Springfield Street.** The house at 220 West Springfield (on the right next to the new building on the corner; *photo*) is another example of one whose lot line is the diagonal city–BWP boundary. Note that this house is two bays wide in front (the bowfront counts as one bay) and that its side wall and that of the new building are not at right angles to the front walls.

Front of
220 West Springfield Street

19 **Return to Columbus Avenue, turn left, go to Massachusetts Avenue, and go around the Harriet Tubman House on the corner to the parking lot behind it.** Note that 220 West Springfield is three bays wide at the rear (*photo*) because it is built on the diagonal city–BWP boundary line.

20 **Return to and cross Columbus Avenue, turn right, turn left on Wellington Street, and go up to Southwest Corridor Park.**

RAILROADS

The first railroads serving Boston opened in 1835. These railroads had been allowed to choose the routes on which they entered

◆ the city and two of them—the Boston & Providence (on the alignment of today's Amtrak) and the Boston & Worcester (on the line of the present commuter rail next to the Mass Pike)—chose to build their tracks across Back Bay, crossing approximately at the location of the present Back Bay station (*see 1835 and current street maps*). The tracks were laid on raised embankments, which were a further impediment

Back of
220 West Springfield Street

to sewage outflow (see p. 78). An *1839 engraving*, drawn looking up the Boston & Providence tracks toward the State House with a Boston & Worcester train departing at the left, gives a good idea of the height of these embankments. Both railroads had their depots on made land—the Boston & Providence just west of Church Street and the Boston & Worcester in South Cove (*see 1835 map* and Walk 9, ◆ p. 138).

1839 engraving of trains crossing in Back Bay

The location of the railroad tracks had a significant impact on the South End. The tracks defined its northern boundaries and also, since bridges crossed the tracks on only the streets from Arlington to Dartmouth (see p. 80), affected its street plan. In 1860 the city decided to extend two new diagonals parallel to the Boston & Providence tracks—Columbus Avenue on the south side, starting at Park Square and running to the South End, and Huntington Avenue on the north side, starting at the intersection of Boylston and Clarendon Streets (Copley Square) and continuing into Roxbury. All the streets northwest of Tremont were to intersect Columbus or Warren Avenues at right angles, which is why there is now a bend at the north end of most of these streets (*see current street map*).

Over the years, some changes have been made in the tracks themselves. After the Boston & Providence was taken over by the New York, New Haven & Hartford in the 1890s, the latter railroad built South Station in 1897–1899 (see Walk 9, ◆ p. 142). The Providence tracks were then rerouted to South Station on the alignment of the former Boston & Worcester tracks. The section of Providence tracks north of the former crossing was discontinued, and the Providence depot in Park Square closed. For many years the land on either side of the Boston & Albany (successor to the Boston & Worcester) tracks between Exeter and Dalton Streets was the Boston & Albany rail yards—(*see current street map and 1934 aerial* in Walk 6, p. 106). The development of this land as the Prudential Center did not begin until the late 1950s (*see 1983 aerial* in Walk 6, p. 106). Then, after community opposition forced plans for a Southwest Expressway to be abandoned in the 1970s, the highway funds were applied to mass transit, permitting a relocation of the MBTA Orange Line next to Amtrak (on the alignment of the former Boston & Providence) and the creation of Southwest Corridor Park over and next to the tracks.

21 **Turn right on Southwest Corridor Park** (note the view of the two John Hancock towers ahead of you), **turn left on West Newton Street (the first street that cuts across the park), and go down to St. Botolph Street.**

HUNTINGTON AVENUE LANDS

As you can see when comparing an *1871 map* of Back Bay with the *current street map*, the area of St. Botolph Street had not yet been filled in 1871. In that year, the BWP, which was having financial difficulties, began to sell, in addition to filled house lots, whole sections of unfilled flats that it would then fill for the buyer. The St. Botolph area was included in the 1871 sale of flats bounded by the Boston & Providence (now Southwest Corridor Park), Camden (now Gainsborough) Street, the line of Huntington Avenue (also not yet filled), and the Boston & Albany (formerly Boston & Worcester, now the Mass Pike) to the trustees of the Huntington Avenue Lands, as this area was originally called (*see 1871 and current street maps*). The BWP was supposed to fill these forty acres by 1872 but actually didn't finish until 1875. St. Botolph Street was then laid out on the made land between the Boston & Providence tracks and Huntington Avenue (*see current street map*) and lots were ready for sale in 1879. Now known as the St. Botolph District, the area was once a locus for musicians, artists, and writers.

22 **Continue down West Newton Street, cross Huntington Avenue, and continue on Belvidere Street (the continuation of West Newton Street) past the Christian Science Center,** noting the Mother Church (*photo*) on your left, **to the corner of Belvidere and Dalton Streets.**

You are now on the former Gravelly Point, the diamond-shaped, marshy peninsula that separated the east and west parts of Back Bay (*see map of made land*). Although original land (*see current street map*), Gravelly Point was so marshy that it needed filling, which the BWP did in the 1880s.

Because many of the buildings on former Gravelly Point are constructed.on fill, they are subject to falling groundwater and rotting foundation piles, a problem that is described in

Christian Science Mother Church

Walk 4, ◆ p. 63. There are several notable instances of rotted foundation piles on former Gravelly Point. The FitzInn parking lot on the corner of Belvidere and Dalton Streets across from the Sheraton is on the site of a row of apartment buildings that was demolished about 1980 because rotted foundation pilings had caused such severe structural damage it was too expensive to repair. And the Christian Science Mother Church has been underpinned.

St. Germain Street

Turn left on Dalton Street and go to St. Germain Street. 23

St. Germain Street (*photo*) is one of the last areas to be filled in eastern Back Bay—the BWP was still making contracts for this area in the mid-1880s—so the houses here are of a later architectural style than most of the others you have seen on this walk.

This is the end of the walk. Nearest T stop—about equidistant between Hynes Convention Center/ICA (Green Line—all branches except "E") and Symphony (Green Line—"E" branch).

W
A
L
K

5

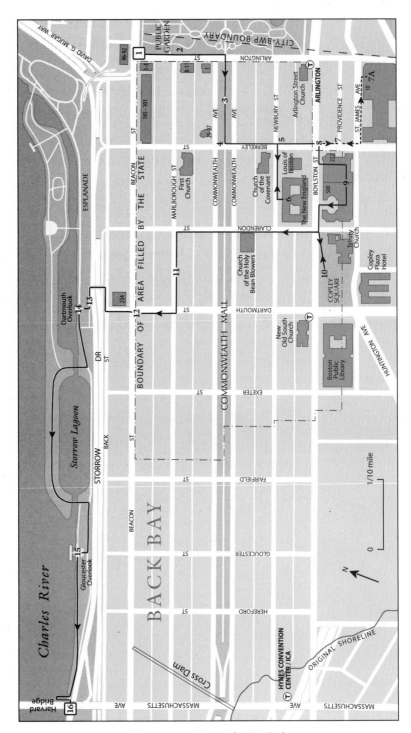

Current street map for Walk 6

Walk 6
BACK BAY AND ESPLANADE

Distance: 2 ½ miles (including optional detour)
Time: 1 ¾ hours
Public Restrooms: Boston Public Library

This walk traces landmaking in the area generally regarded as Back Bay—bounded by Arlington and Beacon Streets, Charlesgate East, and Boylston Street—where you will see the Commonwealth Avenue Mall, noted nineteenth-century churches and other buildings, and streets lined with handsome nineteenth-century town houses. The walk also traces the landmaking that created the Esplanade park along the river in front of Back Bay.

Start at the corner of Beacon and Arlington Streets next to the Public Garden.

1

Nearest T stop—Arlington (Green Line).

Back Bay was originally a large tidal bay on the *back* side of the Boston peninsula (*see map of made land*), hence its name. Filling of Back Bay south of present Boylston Street is explained in Walk 5, while this walk focuses on the landmaking north of Boylston Street (*see current street map*).

MILL DAM

Between 1818 and 1821 a dam was built on the line of Beacon Street across the entire mouth of Back Bay from Charles Street at the foot of the Common to Sewall's Point (today's Kenmore Square). A cross dam was then built on the line of today's Hemenway Street from Gravelly Point, the diamond-shaped, marshy peninsula that divided the eastern and western parts of Back Bay (*see map of made land*), to the main dam (*see current street map*). The purpose of the dams was to power some tide mills and an *1821 plan* shows how the project worked. At high tide water entered the full basin (western Back Bay) through sluice

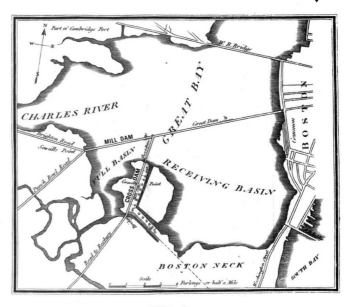

1821 plan

gates, then flowed through raceways on Gravelly Point, powering mills there, then ran into the receiving basin (eastern Back Bay), and finally drained back into the Charles River at low tide. A fifty-foot-wide road, later called Western Avenue, was constructed on top of the Mill Dam—the forerunner of today's Beacon Street.

The Mill Dam had been built by the Boston & Roxbury Mill Corporation (B&RMC), which by 1824 had been authorized to increase the width of the

dam from fifty to two hundred feet. In the mid-1840s the B&RMC constructed a seawall two hundred feet north of the dam from about Brimmer Street, where the made land on the Beacon Hill Flat terminated at

1852 map

that time (see Walk 4, ♦ p. 66), to about today's Clarendon Street and filled the flats behind it with mud. About 1850 some B&RMC shareholders bought lots on this made land and built eight adjoining houses. These houses are shown on details from an *1852 map* (they are the westernmost group of houses. Note also that the seawall extended further than the fill behind it) and from an *1850*

1850 bird's-eye view of the Mill Dam

bird's-eye view (the houses are in the foreground). Note that these houses faced the
unfilled flats of Back Bay. Two of these
houses still remain at 93–94 Beacon Street,
across from where you are now (*photo*. Note
that 92 and 95–96 are in the same location
but not the same buildings as the originals
and 97–99 were demolished to make room
for Embankment Road, now David G.
Mugar Way).

93–94 Beacon Street

BACK BAY PROJECT

By the time the houses at 93–94 Beacon
Street were built in 1849, Back Bay had become very polluted by the sewage emptying
into it from surrounding areas. For most of
the 1800s, Boston sewers discharged raw sewage at the nearest shoreline from
where it was supposed to be carried away by the outgoing tide. In Back Bay,
however, the Mill Dam and also two railroad tracks that had been built across
the receiving basin in the 1830s (see Walk 5, ♦ p. 84) prevented the sewage
from being flushed away. A famous 1849 city report called Back Bay a "great
cesspool" with a "greenish scum many yards wide" along the shore and the surface beyond "bubbling like a cauldron with the noxious gases that are explod-
ing from the corrupting mass below." The solution, most agreed, was to fill
Back Bay and develop the made land as a residential area. It took several years,
however, for the owners of flats in Back Bay—the state, the B&RMC, and the
Boston Water Power Company (BWP), which had operated the mills since
1832, (note that the city was *not* a participant)—to work out an agreement. The
state finally signed indentures with the B&RMC and the BWP in 1854, opening the way for the BWP to start filling its flats in 1855 (see Walk 5, ♦ p. 78).

The state and the BWP divided the four hundred acres of remaining
unfilled flats south of the Mill Dam (Beacon Street). The state got about one
hundred acres in the area now bounded by Arlington and Beacon Streets, a
line between Exeter and Fairfield Streets, and the line of Providence Street
from Exeter to Berkeley Street and of Boylston Street from Berkeley to
Arlington (*see current street map*), and the BWP got the other three hundred
acres. The state was required to pay for its filling from sales of made land, so,
to get the project started, in 1857 it sold the flats for the entire block on
Beacon Street from Arlington to Berkeley—site of the houses now at
101–145 Beacon—to the owners of the two westernmost houses on the Mill
Dam (see p. 90). In 1858 the state contracted with two railroad men to have
its flats filled with gravel, as was also required.

The appearance of Back Bay in 1858 just before the state started filling its
flats is shown an *1858 photo*. The photo was taken from the dome of the State

1858 photo of the Mill Dam and Back Bay

House, a favorite vantage point in the 1800s, looking down the Mill Dam toward the hills of Brookline. You can see the B&RMC's fill on the north side of the dam and, in the distance, the cross dam extending from Gravelly Point to the main dam with two tide-powered mills on it. Closer in are the exposed flats of Back Bay, a line of trees on what became Arlington Street, the rather barren Public Garden, and then, on the nearer side of a row of trees on Charles Street, the Common.

The gravel for Back Bay was brought by rail, most of it from Needham, where it was dug by steam "excavators" (shovels). An *1858 engraving* from *Ballou's Pictorial* shows a steam shovel in action— as a gravel train was pulled past it, the excavator would swing, filling each car with just two shovel fulls. Once loaded,

1858 engraving of loading gravel in Needham

the trains would depart for Back Bay on tracks that essentially followed the route of today's Riverside branch of the Green Line to about present Kenmore station and then the route of the present commuter rail next to the Mass Pike from the Yawkey to the Back Bay station. From there the contractors built spur tracks to the areas being filled. A *c. 1859 photo* shows a gravel train in Back Bay—the cars dumped sideways and the gravel was leveled by horse-drawn scrapers.

2   **Start down Arlington Street next to the Public Garden.**
Note that most of the buildings on the opposite side of Arlington at numbers 1–3, 8–11, and 1 Commonwealth Avenue were built about 1860, soon after this area was filled.

c. 1859 photo of gravel train in Back Bay

WEST EDGE OF PUBLIC GARDEN

One narrow strip of the Back Bay project was filled by the city—the west edge of the Public Garden. When the city filled the rest of the Public Garden in the 1830s (see Walk 5, ♦ p. 73), the park's western boundary was neither perpendicular to the Mill Dam nor on the line of present Arlington Street because it was on the line that divided the city's flats from those of the BWP (*see current street map*). The flats west of that line became the state's property in its 1854 division with the BWP (see p. 91). In 1856 the state gave the city the triangular strip of flats next to the Public Garden needed to make the western boundary of the park perpendicular to the Mill Dam; in return, the city was to fill half of Arlington Street. In 1858, the city decided, over protests from the state, to fill this strip and the street with "clean ashes." (After coal came into common use for heating and cooking about 1840, the city had instituted ash collection—much like trash collection today—and, always needing a place to dispose the ashes, often used them as fill.) Knowing that ashes were used on this strip explains a famous Winslow Homer *1859*

1859 Winslow Homer engraving of scavengers in Back Bay

engraving of scavengers in Back Bay. The scavengers are clearly in what is now the Public Garden, sorting through the ashes for things not fully incinerated. Behind them, the man in a horse-drawn tip cart is on Arlington Street, and behind him you can see the smoke stack of a gravel train in Back Bay. The buildings on the right are on the Mill Dam (Beacon Street), which, lined with trees, recedes into the distance. Although this strip of the Public Garden was the only part of Back Bay to be filled with trash, the Homer engraving is probably responsible for the common misconception that all Back Bay was filled with "hoopskirts and oyster shells."

3   **Cross Arlington Street at Commonwealth Avenue and go down the Commonwealth Avenue Mall.**

COMMONWEALTH AVENUE
The street plan for Back Bay was determined before the state began filling in 1858. From the outset of the project, it had been intended that the central east-west avenue—now Commonwealth Avenue—would be wider than then other streets. In 1856 the state increased the width of this street to 200 feet, which, with the required 20-foot setback for buildings on either side, made the total width 240 feet. The center one hundred feet was to be an ornamental walk, as it still is (*see current street map*).

The reason for devoting so much land to this grand, French-style boulevard—land that could otherwise have been sold as house lots—was to attract upper-middle-class residents. As in the South End before it (see Walk 5, ♦ p. 81, and Walk 10, ♦ p. 152), the "hidden agenda" of the Back Bay project was to create an attractive residential area that would keep upper-middle-class Yankees, who were valued by the city as both tax payers and voters, to remain in the city to counter the Irish, who were pouring into Boston at that time.

4   **Stop at Berkeley Street.**
Although Back Bay was intended as a high-class neighborhood, the made land was required to be sold at public auction because that would presumably get the best price, so theoretically anyone with sufficient money could live in Back Bay. Nonetheless, the state commissioners of the project tried to sell to the

25–27 Commonwealth Avenue

"right sort." For example, when they sold two lots on the northeast corner of Commonwealth Avenue and Berkeley Street at below market price in May 1860 before auctions were mandated, they justified it by saying that such sales to "eligible parties" would induce similar people to buy in Back Bay. It thus seems ironic that these same lots that were sold at too low a price in 1860 became the site of two houses built in

c. 1866 photo of the Mill Dam and Back Bay

1861 at 25–27 Commonwealth Avenue (*photo*)—across from where you are—which in 1998 were converted into four condominiums that then sold for three million dollars per unit!

By 1861 filling of the state's flats extended beyond Clarendon Street and by 1871 almost all the state's flats had been filled (*see 1861 and 1871 maps* in Walk 5, pp. 79 and 80). A *photo* taken *about 1866* from the dome of the State House, the same vantage point as the *1858 photo* (see p. 92), makes an interesting comparison with it and shows the progress of the landmaking. In the *c. 1866 photo* you can see the newly made land in Back Bay and the buildings constructed on

1869 photo of Back Bay

it, especially those on Arlington Street, most of which still exist and which you passed earlier on this walk. Note the opening for Marlborough Street and the empty lot at the corner of Berkeley and Marlborough Streets where First Church, to your right, is today. The absence of the church dates this photograph, which is often misdated c. 1875. Since the church was constructed in 1867–1868, this photo clearly was taken before that.

5   **Go up the east side of Berkeley Street to Newbury Street.**

Across Berkeley Street on the northwest corner of Berkeley and Newbury Streets, note the Church of the Covenant, which was completed in 1866 and is shown in an *1869 photo* of Back Bay, also taken from the dome of the State House. This photo also shows the steeple of First Church at the far right, the buildings on Arlington Street, the wide expanse of Commonwealth Avenue, and the Arlington Street Church at the corner of Arlington and Boylston Streets, erected in 1860 as one of the very first buildings on the state's made land in Back Bay.

Diagonally across from you, on the southwest corner of Berkeley and Newbury, is the building now occupied by Louis of Boston (*photo*). In 1860 the state had noted that the greatest demand in Back Bay was for lots facing the Public Garden or the Commonwealth Avenue Mall and that open blocks would enhance the value and character of the surrounding area. So in 1861 the state donated the eastern third of the block

Museum of Natural History
(Louis of Boston)

bounded by Berkeley, Boylston, Clarendon, and Newbury Streets to the Boston Society for Natural History and the western two-thirds to the newly incorporated Massachusetts Institute of Technology (MIT), stipulating that both institutions erect buildings covering no more than one-third of their land. The Museum of Natural History building—now Louis of Boston—was built in 1862 and the first MIT building, later named the Rogers Building, erected in 1864 facing Boylston Street. (MIT moved to its present location in Cambridge in 1916, but the Rogers Building and the Walker Building, which was built next to the former in 1883, remained until 1939, when they were demolished for The New England building, which you will visit next.) The Museum of Natural History continued to occupy the building on Berkeley Street until 1947 when, having become the Boston Museum of Science and having sold the Back Bay building, it moved out, occupying its new site on the first Charles River Dam in 1950 (see Walk 3, ◆ p. 56). The Museum of Natural History building then became a clothing store—Bonwit Teller from 1947 to 1987 and Louis of Boston since 1988.

You can see both the Museum of Natural History and first MIT building in the *1869 photo* between the Arlington Street Church and the Church of the Covenant, but they are shown more clearly at the right-hand side of a detail from an *1870 bird's-eye view* of Back Bay from the west with Clarendon Street in the foreground and the Public Garden in the background. In this view, you can also see the Arlington Street Church, the Church of the Covenant, and First Church. Note the blank ends of buildings awaiting the construction of the ones adjoining them.

1870 bird's-eye view of Back Bay

Turn right (west) on Newbury Street and go into The New England building (open Monday–Saturday 10–10, Sunday 11–7, subject to change). In the lobby of The New England are four historical dioramas, including one about the Boylston Street Fishweir, one about filling Back Bay, and one about the Museum of Natural History building.

BOYLSTON STREET FISHWEIR

The Boylston Street Fishweir is Boston's most famous archaeological site and is so-named because it was first discovered in 1913 when the subway was being constructed down Boylston Street. The fishweir is a network of vertical stakes with horizontal branches laid against or woven through them. At high tide fish would swim in over the weir but at low tide they would be trapped by it and then collected by the Native Americans in the area. Recent research has found that the fishweir may not have been a single structure but perhaps several smaller structures and that the weirs were built 5,300–3,700 years ago when the sea level was much lower than it is now. The rising ocean deposited sixteen feet of silt on top of the weirs and filling Back Bay added eighteen feet of fill on top of that, so the weirs are protected except in the case of excavations that go deeper than thirty-four feet. The fishweirs were investigated in 1939 when the building you are in was being constructed for the New England Mutual Life Insurance Company, in 1986 during construction of 500 Boylston Street, in 1958 for a building at Boylston and Clarendon Streets that preceded the one at 500 Boylston Street, and in 1946 when the first Hancock Tower on Berkeley and Stuart Streets was being built. You will note that all these sites are between Berkeley and Clarendon Streets, though the fishweirs are thought to underlie much of Back Bay.

The diorama of the fishweir is based on results from the 1939 and 1946 archaeological investigations and on modern ethnographic examples. The 2500 B.C. date was based on radiocarbon analysis of the fishweir stakes as were the dates of 5,300–3,700 years ago cited above, and the two do not disagree, since 2500 B.C. was, of course, about 4,500 years ago. The heart shape of the trap is not supported by recent research, however, which has envisioned the fishweirs as lines of stakes.

The diorama of filling Back Bay may very well have been based on the *c. 1859 photo* on p. 93. The scene is meant to be a view from the site of the building you are in looking toward the Public Garden and the Common, but, as you can see, there are some inaccuracies. Filling progressed westward from Arlington Street, so there would not have been water between here and the Public Garden (*see 1861 map* in Walk 5, p. 79), and the latter was not edged with a seawall. On the other hand, the railroad cars dumping sideways and the horse-drawn levelers seem to be based on historical fact.

The diorama featuring the Museum of Natural History is about the building you saw at the corner of Berkeley and Newbury Streets. The scene clearly represents 1863, for the museum (1862) has been completed and the foundation of the first MIT building (1864) behind it has been laid. The scene also suggests that by that date the buildings on Commonwealth Avenue extended as far as Berkeley Street (compare with a detail from an *1870 bird's-eye view*) and those on the water side of Beacon Street (the Mill Dam) to Dartmouth Street (compare with the *1863–1869 photo* on p. 101). Note the gravel train in the vicinity of Dartmouth Street.

7 **Exit from The New England building onto Newbury Street, turn right, cross Berkeley Street and turn right, cross Boylston Street, and go to Providence Street.**

Providence Street marks the southern boundary of the state's territory in Back Bay. It's ironic that Providence Street only still exists in the block between Berkeley and Arlington Streets where Boylston Street was the boundary of the state's land (see above) whereas Providence Street has been discontinued in the blocks between Berkeley and Exeter Streets, where it *was* the boundary (*see current street map*).

To see some maps that show Boston's landmaking, take the optional detour below. Otherwise, skip ahead to 8.

Optional detour. Continue up Berkeley Street and cross St. James Avenue, turn left, and go in the entrance of 10 St. James Avenue closest to Arlington Street (second glass canopy).   7A

Inlaid in the lobby floor, on either side of a large map of modern Boston, are maps that show the land area of Boston in 1630, 1795, 1852, 1880, 1916, 1934, 1950, and 1995 (based on maps in Alex Krieger and David Cobb with Amy Turner, eds., *Mapping Boston* [Cambridge, Mass.: The MIT Press, 1999], 16–19).

Return to Berkeley and Providence Streets.   7

From the corner of Berkeley and Providence Streets, return on Berkeley to Boylston Street.   8

Note the good views from Berkeley Street of the Museum of Natural History building and the Church of the Covenant.

Turn left on Boylston Street and go into the Boylston Street entrance of the 222 Berkeley Street building (first entrance on left, opposite a boy-on-a-dolphin graphic inlaid in the pavement. Open M–F, 8–6). Go straight down the corridor and turn right into the corridor labeled "↑ 500 Boylston St." Go to the display panels on the right titled "Boston's Back Bay" and "The Fishweir."   9

These panels have some interesting historical photos of Back Bay and an explanation of the Boylston Street Fishweir. Note that the fishweir here is depicted as a line of stakes, as it probably was, rather than as a heart-shaped trap, as shown in the diorama in The New England building.

Exit from the 500 Boylston Street building, turn left on Boylston Street, cross Clarendon Street, enter Copley Square, and go at least as far as the fountain on Boylston Street.   10

1880s photo of Back Bay

The area of Copley Square was filled in the 1860s. In 1869 a huge coliseum was built on the site now occupied by the Copley Plaza Hotel for a National Peace Jubilee to celebrate peace at the end of the Civil War. You can see this coliseum in the *1869 photo* behind the steeple of the Arlington Street Church. In 1864 the BWP had been required to donate the site used for the coliseum as the location for an Institute of Fine Arts (forerunner of today's Museum of Fine Arts) to match the state's donation of the block for the Museum of Natural History and MIT buildings (see p. 96). The Institute of Fine Arts opened in 1876 and remained in Copley Square until it moved to its present location on the Fenway in 1909 (see Walk 7, ◆ p. 117). Copley Square is the site of some notable buildings—Trinity Church (1877), New Old South Church (1875), and the Boston Public Library (1895). The first two can be seen in a *photo* taken from the dome of the State House in the *1880s*, which shows the filling of Back Bay up to that time and makes an interesting comparison with the *c. 1866 and 1869 photos* from the same vantage point.

For many years Huntington Avenue ran diagonally through Copley Square from its origin at Clarendon Street (from the northeast corner of the fountain you can look right down Huntington, which runs to the left of the Boston Public Library), leaving the square a rather uninteresting triangle (*see 1934 aerial photo* on p. 106). It was only in the late 1960s that Copley Square was redesigned and became a real square.

11 **Retrace your route to Clarendon Street and turn left.** At the southwest corner of Clarendon Street and Commonwealth Avenue, note the "Church of the Holy Bean Blowers" (1872), as it is commonly called in a joking reference to the trumpet-blowing angels at the corners of the tower, which you can also see in the *1880s photo*. **Continue down Clarendon to Marlborough Street and turn left.**

In contrast to the South End (see Walk 5, ◆ p. 81), Back Bay *did* become the fashionable residential area that had been envisioned. This was aided by many building restrictions—lots could not be used for "mechanical or manufacturing" or, on Commonwealth Avenue, "mercantile" purposes. Many prominent Bostonians moved to Back Bay in the late 1800s, living in houses that, according to the restrictions, had to be at least three stories high, be set back a prescribed distance, and have no more than a five-foot projection in front. But by the mid-1900s, Back Bay houses had begun to deteriorate—many of the Boston Brahmins had moved to the suburbs and their houses and mansions had been converted into rooming houses, apartments, or doctors' offices. Since then, however, there has been a resurgence of single-family ownership and, although the upper class no longer predominates and many original houses and mansions are still rental units or owned by institutions, Back Bay is considered one of the most prestigious residential neighborhoods in the city. The residential character of Back Bay is particularly evident on Marlborough Street, down which you are going.

1863–1869 photo of B&RMC seawall

Continue down Marlborough, turn right on Dartmouth Street, and go 12
to the southwest corner of Dartmouth and Beacon Streets.

BOSTON & ROXBURY MILL CORPORATION (B&RMC) SEAWALL
While the state and BWP were filling their parts of Back Bay, the B&RMC
was also required to do some filling. According to its 1854 agreement with ◆
the state (see p. 91), the B&RMC was to extend the seawall it had started two
hundred feet north of the Mill Dam (see p. 90) all
the way across Back Bay to Brookline and fill the
flats between the seawall and the dam (Beacon
Street). Between 1859 and 1863 the B&RMC built
the seawall and filled the flats as far as the cross
dam, which intersected the Mill Dam between
present Hereford Street and Massachusetts Avenue
(*see current street map*). (The B&RMC filled the wall
and flats west of that point between 1881 and
1887—see Walk 8, ◆ p. 126.) You can see the
progress of the B&RMC's wall and fill on the *1858,
c. 1866, and 1880s photos* of the Mill Dam/Beacon
Street from the dome of the State House. You can
also see the seawall and fill in a *photo* taken sometime *between 1863 and 1869*, which shows people

234 Beacon Street

sitting on the wall and the fill in the foreground. In the middle distance, the
new buildings on either side of Beacon Street (the former Mill Dam) extend
as far as Dartmouth Street; at the right are some old buildings on the dam.
The photo can be dated by the presence of the building on the northeast corner of Beacon and Dartmouth Streets—the building you are now viewing
diagonally across from you at 234 Beacon Street (*photo* [the second floor oriel
bay and balcony are later additions])—which was built in 1863, and the
absence of the original building across from it on the northwest corner, which
was not constructed until 1869.

1894 photo from the Harvard Bridge at high tide

1894 photo from the Harvard Bridge at low tide

13   **Go toward the river on Dartmouth Street.** The street behind the houses on Beacon Street is Back Street, which was laid out next to the seawall as a service alley for these houses, which it still is. **Go up the footbridge over Storrow Drive, stopping on the north (river) side of the bridge.**

ESPLANADE

From the north side of the footbridge across Storrow Drive you have a view of the three stages of landmaking that created the Esplanade, which are explained below—the drive is on the part filled in 1907–1909 (you can see the 1860s B&RMC seawall next to it), the balustrade of the Dartmouth Overlook (ahead of you) is on the shore of the 1930s widening, and the island on the other side of the lagoon is 1950–1951 fill.

1908 photo of filling the Boston Embankment from the Harvard Bridge

The first Charles River Dam, built in 1905–1910, changed the river from a tidal estuary to a freshwater basin maintained at a constant level in order to keep the smelly polluted flats in the river always covered with water (see Walk 3, ♦ p. 55). *Photos* taken in *1894* from the Harvard (Massachusetts Avenue) Bridge show the ten-foot difference between high and low tide and the flats visible at low tide before the dam was built. The photos also show the B&RMC seawall and Back Street next to it, behind the houses on Beacon Street. The dam project not only created today's Charles River Basin, but also involved filling a narrow park along the Boston side of the basin. Called the Boston Embankment, the section along Back Bay was to be one hundred feet

1910 photo of the Boston Embankment from the Harvard Bridge

1919 photo of the Boston Embankment from Embankment Road

wide. Filling of this section was done in 1907–1909, as you can see in a *1908 photo* taken from the Harvard Bridge. The photo illustrates that, contrary to past landmaking practice, the seawall—of poured concrete, a departure from the customary granite blocks—was constructed at the same time the embankment was filled, in this case with material dredged from the river. (The big trench you see down the center of the embankment was for the Boston Marginal Conduit, a large sewer.) Note that the B&RMC seawall is visible on the right-hand side of this photo. The finished embankment is shown in a *1910 photo* taken from the same vantage point as the *1908 photo*. Note that the final line of fill reached to the top of the B&RMC seawall, completely covering it. Another view of the narrow embankment filled in 1907–1909 is a *1919 photo* taken from Embankment Road (now David G. Mugar Way) looking upriver. On the other side of the river, note the dome of the main building of MIT, which had just moved to Cambridge from its Back Bay location.

As explained in Walk 4, ♦ p. 67, the Charles River Basin did not at first become the "water park" that had been envisioned, and in the early 1930s the Esplanade was widened and new recreational facilities added. Filling of the Back Bay section began in 1931, again with material dredged from the river, and was generally completed by *1934*. A *photo* taken that year from the Harvard (Massachusetts Avenue) Bridge, but to the left of the *1908 and 1910 photos*, shows the new shoreline sloping down to the water's edge rather than ending in a seawall. And a *1935 photo* from Embankment Road (David G. Mugar Way), the same vantage point as the *1919 photo*, clearly shows, in comparison with the earlier photo, the doubled width of the Esplanade as well as

1935 photo of the Esplanade from Embankment Road

the major recreational improvement in the Back Bay section—a lagoon between Exeter and Fairfield Streets. The improvements to the Esplanade in the 1930s appear also in a *1934 aerial photo,* which shows that the narrow strip filled in 1907–1909 has been more than doubled by the 1930s fill and lagoon.

1934 photo of the Esplanade from the Harvard Bridge

1934 aerial photo of the Charles River Basin and Boston

1983 aerial photo of the Charles River Basin and Boston

As also explained in Walk 4, ♦ p. 67, the highway along the river omitted from the 1930s widening of the Esplanade was constructed after World War II and named Storrow Drive. The drive was constructed on the part of the Esplanade filled in 1907–1909, and, to compensate for the land taken, some islands were filled along the river, forming lagoons adjoining the one created in the 1930s. This filling was done in 1950–1951 with dirt trucked in from the suburbs, and the results can be seen on a *1983 aerial photo*, especially in comparison with the *1934 aerial photo*. As part of the project, Storrow Drive was required to be depressed to at least a foot and a half above the river, that is, below the level of the Esplanade. When the Esplanade was cut down, the seawall built by the B&RMC was revealed, and that is why you can now see it next to Storrow Drive.

Go straight ahead to the Dartmouth Overlook (the steps at the water's edge).   14

This overlook was added in the 1930s (you can see it east of the lagoon on the   ♦
1934 aerial photo). It is similar in style to Commissioners Landing, which was built at the same time on the section of the Esplanade in front of the Beacon Hill Flat (see Walk 4, ♦ p. 69).

Go west (toward Massachusetts Avenue), noting the 1860s B&RMC sea-   15
wall visible on the far side of Storrow Drive. **Cross the first bridge over the lagoon, go on the outer side of the Storrow Lagoon**—the 1930s lagoon between Exeter and Fairfield Streets—**take the bridge back to the 1930s fill, and go to the Gloucester Overlook.**

Note how the 1930s shoreline sloped down to the water's edge. At the Gloucester Overlook, also constructed in the 1930s (*see 1934 aerial photo*),   ♦
view the 1948 memorial to the Storrows—it's a compass and a map of the Charles River.

Continue west (toward Massachusetts Avenue) and go up the foot-   16
bridge to the Harvard (Massachusetts Avenue) Bridge.

At the top, go a short distance out on the bridge and compare the view with that in the *1934 photo* from about the same spot (note how the westbound part of Storrow Drive occupies much of the Esplanade filled in the 1930s). Then, moving toward the Boston end of the bridge, compare the view with that in the *1894, 1908, and 1910 photos* (note that Storrow Drive is on the Boston Embankment created in 1907–1909).

This is the end of the walk. Nearest T station—Hynes Convention Center/ICA (Green Line—all branches except "E").

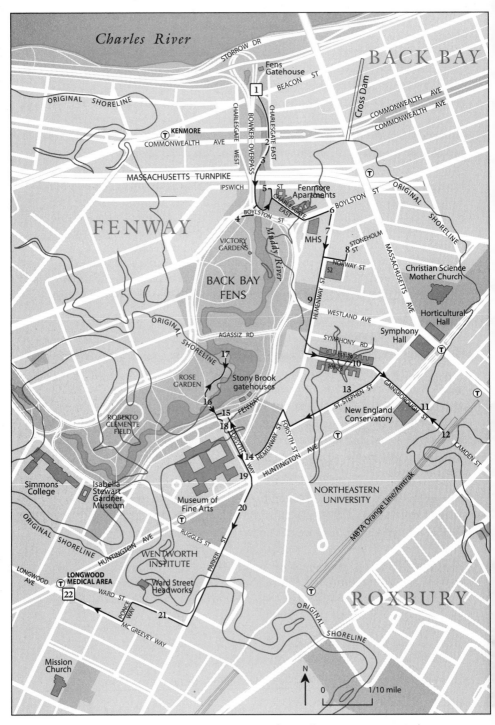

Current street map for Walk 7

Walk 7
BACK BAY FENS, FENWAY, AND MISSION HILL

Distance: 3 miles
Time: 1 3/4 hours
Public Restrooms: Museum of Fine Arts (West Wing entrance)
Note: This walk includes a flight of stairs.

This walk covers the landmaking that created the Back Bay Fens—the first Boston park designed by Frederick Law Olmsted—the Fenway area around it with its late nineteenth- and early twentieth-century buildings, and also some sites related to landmaking in the Mission Hill area. As you can see from the *made land and current street maps*, the Back Bay Fens and surrounding areas were created by filling in the western part of Back Bay; other landmaking in the western Back Bay area is covered in Walk 8.

Start on the north side of the bridge over the Muddy River on Beacon   1
Street between Charlesgate East and Charlesgate West.
Nearest T stop—Kenmore (Green Line—"B," "C," and "D" branches).

Note the small arched stone footbridge (*photo*) over the Muddy River to the north (toward the Charles River). The Muddy River disappears into a conduit on the other side of this bridge. On the Beacon Street bridge move east (toward downtown) far enough to see the Fens gatehouse (*photo*) on the other side of the ramp leading to Storrow Drive, and note how far the

Footbridge at Beacon Entrance

Fens gatehouse

gatehouse is from the edge of the Charles. (Both the gatehouse and footbridge are actually related to a landmaking project that will be discussed later on the walk, but, since the walk will not return to this area, they are best viewed now.)

♦   BACK BAY FENS

In the 1870s Boston decided to establish a public park system. The very first park in this system, begun in 1878, was the Back Bay Fens. The Fens was not originally intended as a recreation area, however, but as a solution to a sewer-

♦   age problem. At that time the sewers that served the Stony Brook valley (where the Orange Line/Amtrak tracks now run through Roxbury and Jamaica Plain) and the parts of Brookline bordering the Muddy River drained into those two streams, which then carried the raw sewage into the full basin—the western part of Back Bay (*see 1836 map*)—reportedly making it "the filthiest marsh and mud flats to be found anywhere in Massachusetts. . . .; a body of water so foul that . . . no one will go within half a mile of in summer unless of necessity, so great is the stench arising therefrom." The city planned to use the new park as a storage basin for excess water from the Muddy River and Stony Brook sewers, which often overflowed during heavy rains. The city engineer envisioned this storage basin as a stone-lined reservoir, but in 1878,

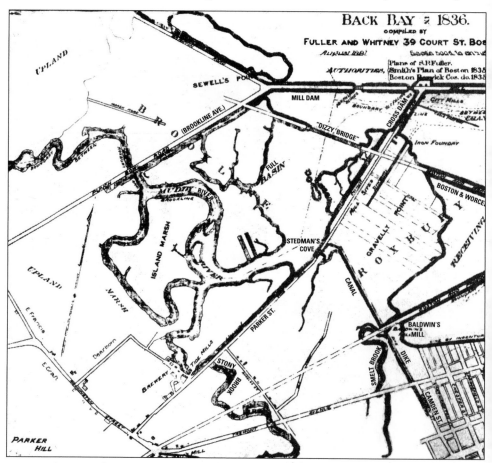

1836 map

after the park commissioners rejected the winning plan in their competition for the design of the new park, they turned to Frederick Law Olmsted, the well known landscape architect, who had already consulted with them in 1875 and 1876 on park selection.

Olmsted had a very different idea for the park, shown in an *1879 plan*. He planned to make the storage basin by creating a salt marsh. A waterway was to be constructed through the park by dredging and filling and its banks were

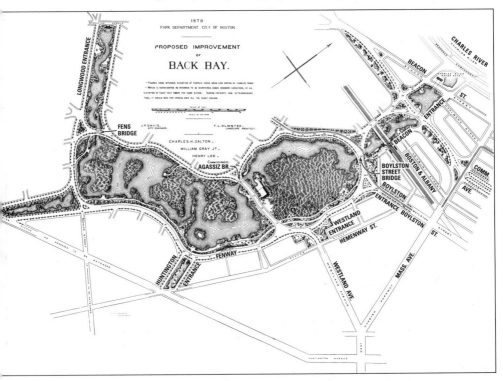

1879 plan

then to be planted with "sedgy" vegetation that could survive in both salt and brackish water. And the Stony Brook and Muddy River sewers were to be extended directly to the Charles, bypassing the new park. Olmsted's plan was affected by the shape of the park and the six "entrances" (the leglike extensions on the *1879 plan*) that had already been determined by the city as had the bending of Commonwealth Avenue at Massachusetts Avenue so it wouldn't have to cross the Boston & Albany tracks (a decision often erroneously attributed to Olmsted).

Work on the Olmsted plan began in 1880 with filling at what was called the Beacon entrance, which is where you are now. Note on the *1879 plan* that the entrance originally ended just north of Beacon Street—the land north of that was made later. Note also how the Bowker Overpass has obliterated the design of the entrance (compare the *1879 plan* with a *c. 1966 aerial photo of Charlesgate*).

c. 1966 aerial photo of Charlesgate

2 **Cross Beacon Street and go along the Muddy River to the south (far) side of the inbound roadway of Commonwealth Avenue.**

Note where the river passes under the bridges on Commonwealth Avenue and that the waterway is in essentially the same location as on the *1879 plan*. The Commonwealth Avenue bridges, however, with their distinctive balustrades, were built when the avenue was widened in 1925 (compare Commonwealth Avenue on the *1879 plan* and the *c. 1966 aerial photo*).

3 **Take the sidewalk next to the down ramp from the overpass and go up the ramp.**

Note the large stone bridge ahead across the Muddy River. As you cross the turnpike, note that the tracks next to the turnpike are on the alignment of the original Boston & Worcester, later Boston & Albany, Railroad and approximately the location of a bridge over the full basin known as the "Dizzy Bridge" because of its lack of railings and widely spaced trestles (*see 1836 and current street maps*). On the other side of the turnpike, note the parapet wall of the stone bridge and that the seams are tinted terra-cotta—the style when the bridge was built in the 1880s.

4 **At the indentation in the parapet wall, cross the roadways and go to the "Back Bay Fens" sign.**

Near the "Back Bay Fens" sign note the victory gardens—a later addition to the Fens.

Go back across Boylston Street and down the path next to the Boylston   5
Street Bridge to Ipswich Street for a view of the bridge (*photo*).

Olmsted envisioned the Boylston
Street Bridge, designed by consulting
architect H. H. Richardson, as especially wide and high to frame a pic-
turesque view of the Fens from
Commonwealth Avenue that would
entice visitors into the park. Now, of
course, the view from Commonwealth Avenue is obscured by the
turnpike, the bridge can be seen only
from the obscurity of Ipswich Street,
and the view into the Fens is obscured
by phragmites—the tall bamboo-like
plants with plumes.

**Boylston Street Bridge
from Ipswich Street**

Go up Charlesgate East past the Fenmore apartments, noting the Massa-   6
chusetts Historical Society (MHS) at the corner of Boylston and the Fenway,
bear left onto Boylston Street, and go to Hemenway Street.

FENWAY AREA
While the Back Bay Fens was being created, the tidal flats and marshes around
it were also being filled, making what is now the Fenway area. The Fenmore
apartments, for example, are on land that was created in 1884–1885 by the
private owners of the flats, who arranged to have them filled with coal ashes
and gravel. The city filled the section of Boylston Street between Hemenway
Street and the Fenway—the original Boylston entrance to the Back Bay Fens
(*see 1879 plan*)—in 1885 with dirt brought by horse-drawn carts.

Turn right on Hemenway Street.   7

CROSS DAM
Hemenway Street was on the alignment of the cross dam (*see current street map*),
a dam built to intersect a longer dam called the Mill Dam, which was constructed in 1818–1821 across the entire mouth of Back Bay on the line of
Beacon Street from Charles Street to today's Kenmore Square. The Mill Dam
dammed off all Back Bay and the cross dam divided it into two basins: a full
basin into which water was taken at high tide and a receiving basin into
which water flowed after running through raceways on Gravelly Point—the
marshy peninsula that divided the western and eastern sections of Back Bay
(*see 1836 map, made land, and current street maps*)—powering mills there.

Turn left on Norway Street and left on Stoneholm Street.   8
Part of Stoneholm Street is on the site of a raceway that was filled in 1885 (*see
1882 and current street maps*).

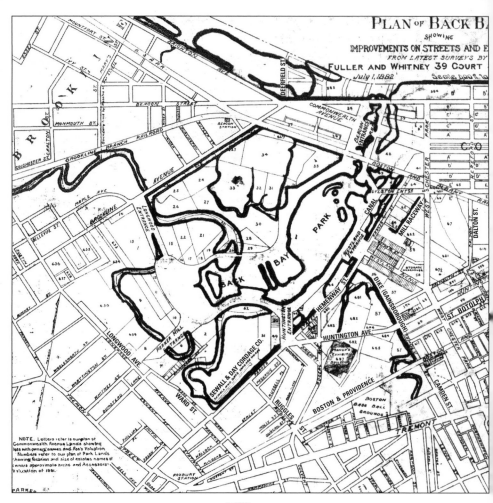

1882 map

9   Retrace your route to Hemenway Street and turn left.

At the corner of Norway and Hemenway note the large orange and red brick and stucco Jacobethan-style building (52 Hemenway Street). It was built in 1892 as a stable for the New Riding Club, which had been attracted to this area by the recently completed bridle paths in the Back Bay Fens and now houses The Badminton and Tennis Club. At Westland Avenue, note the Westland entrance to the Fens. (The Johnson Gates are a 1905 addition—read the plaque for more information.) The intersection of Hemenway and Gainsborough Streets is on the site of Stedman's Cove on the west side of Gravelly Point (*see 1836 and current street maps*).

10   Turn left on Gainsborough Street and go down it.

In the late 1820s a canal was dug across Gravelly Point from Stedman's Cove to Baldwin's Mill, which had been built in 1825 at the mouth of Smelt Brook on the other side of Gravelly Point (*see 1836 map*), to bring more water to power the mill. The canal was contained by a dike on its northeast side, which is now the site of Gainsborough and Camden Streets (*see 1836, 1882, and current street maps*). So, as you go down Gainsborough Street, think canal to your right. The canal as well as the entire area between Hemenway Street and the Orange Line/Amtrak (formerly Boston & Providence) tracks was filled in 1883 (*see 1882 and current street maps*).

On Gainsborough Street, the houses at 108–78 (on the right) and 111–79 (on the left) are red brick bowfront four-family row houses built in the early 1900s, most of them now occupied by students and other renters.

Cross Huntington Avenue and continue down Gainsborough Street.　　11

As you cross Huntington Avenue, note the New England Conservatory of 　♦
Music and Jordan Hall on the southwest corner, both on land made in 1883 when the rest of the Gainsborough area was filled (*see 1882 map*).

At the end of Gainsborough Street, go up the stairs over the Orange　12
Line/Amtrak tracks.

The intersection of Gainsborough Street and the tracks is the site of Baldwin's Mill (see p. 114). From the top of the stairs you can see that, in Lower Roxbury, Gainsborough Street becomes Camden Street, which is also on the site of the dike and next to the former canal (*see 1836 and current street maps*).

Retrace your route on Gainsborough across Huntington, turn left on St.　13
Stephen Street, and go down it.

The St. Stephen Street area was filled in 1883 under the same contract that filled the Gainsborough Street area (see above and *1882 and current street maps*). Most of the 1890s/early 1900s single-family houses and apartment buildings that line the street are now owned by Northeastern University and/or occupied by Northeastern students.

Enter Northeastern University, turn right on Forsyth Street, turn left　14
on Hemenway Street, and go to Forsyth Way.

Forsyth Way is the original Huntington entrance to the Back Bay Fens (*see 1879 plan*). It is also the site of the Commissioners' Channel, dug in the late 1880s to carry storm overflows into the Fens from the Stony Brook sewer that had been extended to the Charles (see p. 111). This arrangement functioned well only until 1897, however, when the entire—and heavily polluted—flow of Stony Brook was routed into the Fens, creating a "foul condition" in the park's waterway. The solution was to build a new Stony Brook conduit (sewer) from the Commissioners' Channel to Charlesgate East, bypassing the Fens altogether. This was done in 1903–1905 and then, when the Boston Marginal Conduit was constructed down the length of the Boston Embankment (now Esplanade) in 1907–1909 during the first Charles River Dam project (*see 1908 photo* in Walk 6, p. 103), the Stony Brook conduit was connected to it. What is called the Fens gatehouse was built on the river over the connection between the Stony Brook and Boston Marginal Conduits—the gatehouse you saw at the beginning of the walk. The Boston Embankment filled in 1907–1909 extended as far as Charlesgate West, so new land was made across the Beacon entrance, and the arched stone footbridge, which you also saw at the beginning of the walk, was constructed over the Muddy River. Once the new Stony Brook conduit had been constructed, completely diverting Stony Brook from the Fens, there was no reason to keep the Commissioners' Channel open, so it was filled and Forsyth Way laid out on the new land.

15　**Turn right on Forsyth Way and cross the Fenway.**

Note that the Fenway is one of the original roadways around the Fens (*see 1879 plan*); it was filled in the early 1880s. Also note the Stony Brook gatehouses to your right. The one closest to you (*photo*), designed by H. H. Richardson and built in 1882, is over the junction of the first Stony Brook conduit and the Fens; it was moved to its present location in 1905 when the second Stony Brook gatehouse was built next to it over the new Stony Brook conduit (see p. 115).

Stony Brook gatehouse

16　**Cross the footbridge into the Fens.**

BACK BAY FENS (REVISITED)

Construction of the Fens according to Olmsted's plan was completed in 1894. The story of the Fens since then has been one of changes to the original plan. These changes began as early as 1904 when, in response to criticisms that the park did not serve recreational needs, filling began of the waterway at the south end near the Fens Bridge (*see 1879 plan*) in order to create a playground. This filling continued for years over strong objections from the Olmsted firm, which felt it was a "savage waste" of a park that had been created, at enormous cost, to be a beautiful landscape. The fill was coal ashes and dirt from excavations, including that for the subway under Boylston Street. This landmaking moved the waterway from the west to the east side of the park (*see 1879 and current street plans*) and created the land that is now Roberto Clemente Field. To your left, you can see the field when the leaves are off the trees. Ahead of you is the rose garden, another change in the Olmsted plan, this one made between 1931 and 1933. And the victory gardens that you saw earlier on the walk are on an area filled in 1910–1911, in order to create a recreational area, with dirt from the excavation of the subway (now Red Line) tunnel under Beacon Hill.

17　**Bear right onto the grass through the war memorial.**

On the right note the arches for the Stony Brook conduits under the Stony Brook gatehouses on the opposite side of the waterway. Between the Vietnam and Korean War memorials, in wintertime when the phragmites are dead,

you can see the Agassiz Bridge (*photo*), built in 1887–1888 as part of the original Olmsted plan (*see 1879 plan*) to carry Agassiz Road over the waterway.

Return across the footbridge to Forsyth Way.   18

FENWAY INSTITUTIONS
After filling of the Fenway area was completed in the 1890s, many cultural and educational institutions moved to the newly made land. The Museum of

Agassiz Bridge

Fine Arts, which you see on the right, moved in 1909 from its earlier location in Copley Square (see Walk 6, ◆ p. 100) to this site, which had been filled in 1885. The Massachusetts Historical Society relocated in 1899 to a building you passed earlier on this walk at the corner of Boylston Street and the Fenway. Other institutions included the Boston Symphony and the Massachusetts Horticultural Society, both of which built new homes on either side of Massachusetts Avenue at Westland Avenue in 1900; the original Christian Science Mother Church in 1894; the New England Conservatory of Music (1902) with Jordan Hall (1904), which you passed at the corner of Gainsborough Street and Huntington Avenue; Mrs. Jack Gardner's Venetian palace, now the Gardner Museum, on the Fenway in 1903; and, further along the Fenway, Simmons College in 1904 (*see current street map*).

Go down Forsyth Way to Huntington Avenue.   19
The section of Huntington Avenue between Forsyth Way and Longwood Avenue (to your right; *see current street map*) was filled in 1883 with gravel brought by railroad—the Boston & Albany built a trestle across Stony Brook so the trains could start filling at the Huntington entrance (now Forsyth Way; see *1882 and current street maps*). An *1884 photo* taken from the Mission Church (*see 1888 map*) shows the newly completed Huntington Avenue extending across the marshes.

1884 photo of the Back Bay Fens

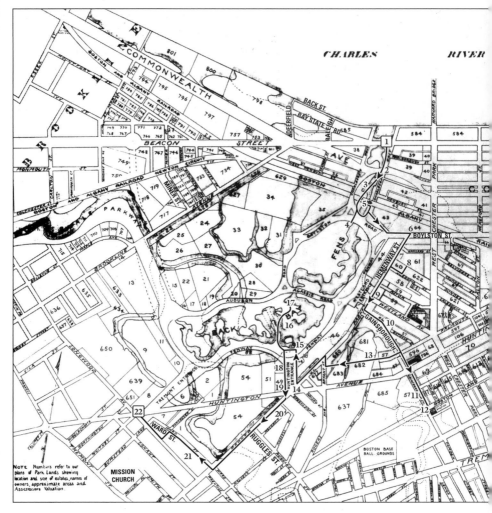

1888 map

20   **Bear right onto Parker Street (the street on the right-hand side of the large striped-brick dormitory with curved walls).**

Parker Street was an early road to Gravelly Point (Hemenway Street was a later extension of it). Where Parker Street crossed Stony Brook there were some tide mills—approximately at the present intersection of Parker and Ward Streets (*see 1836 and current street maps*). The tide mills closed in the early nineteenth century and in 1834 the Sewall and Day Cordage Company established a ropewalk on the site next to a canal that had been dug along to Parker Street from the full basin to Stony Brook (*see 1836 map*). So as you start up Parker Street, think canal to your right (*see 1882 map*). After you cross Ruggles Street, note that Wentworth Institute is located on land made by filling both Stony Brook and the canal (*see 1882 and current street maps*). This filling was done in 1885 after the city solicitor had overruled Sewall and Day's objection to filling the canal. The area was then filled with material brought from Auburndale (a section of suburban Newton) by the Boston & Albany Railroad.

Turn right on Ward Street. 21

The intersection of Parker and Ward Streets is about where the original tide mills were located (see p. 118). Across Ward Street is Mission Main, built on the site of a public housing project of the same name constructed in 1940 with brick buildings similar to those on the other side of Parker Street but "severely distressed" by the 1990s. The original buildings were therefore demolished in 1997 and the project rebuilt with the present houses by a public-private partnership between 1998 and 2002. The site of the Ward Street Headworks (an installation that pumps sewage to the treatment plant at Deer Island), on your right just before Ponce Way, was once part of Stony Brook (*see 1882 and current street maps*). Filling of this area began in 1883 and continued into the 1890s.

Turn left on Ponce Way. From Ponce Way there is a good view of the 22
Mission Church from which the *1884 photo of the Back Bay Fens* was taken, apparently from the octagonal lantern, since the towers weren't added until 1910. **Go right on McGreevey Way to Huntington Avenue.**

Huntington Avenue marks the end of this walk. Nearest T stop—Longwood Medical Area (Green Line—"E" branch).

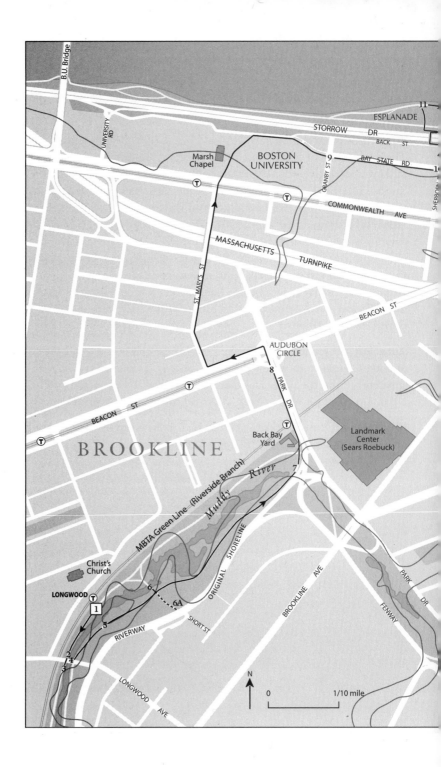

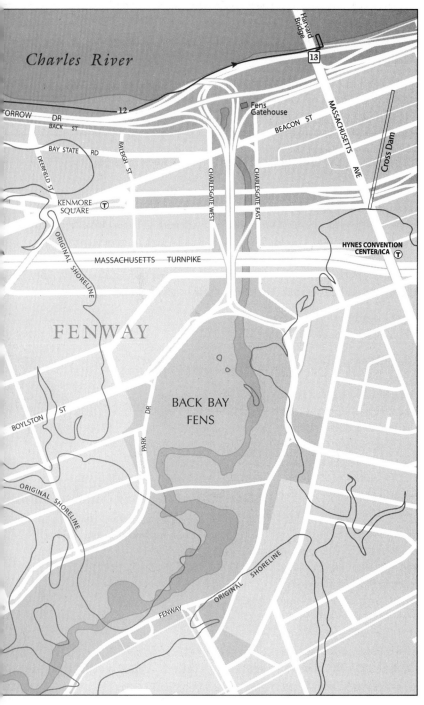

Charles River

12

Harvard Bridge

13

TORROW DR
BACK ST

Fens
Gatehouse

BEACON ST

MASSACHUSETTS AVE

Cross Dam

BAY STATE RD

RALEIGH ST

DEERFIELD ST

CHARLESGATE WEST

CHARLESGATE EAST

KENMORE
SQUARE Ⓣ

ORIGINAL SHORELINE

HYNES CONVENTION
CENTER/ICA Ⓣ

MASSACHUSETTS TURNPIKE

FENWAY

BOYLSTON ST

PARK DR

BACK BAY
FENS

ORIGINAL SHORELINE

ORIGINAL SHORELINE

FENWAY

Current street map for Walk 8

Walk 8

Riverway, Audubon Circle, Bay State Road, and Esplanade

Distance: 2 1/4 miles (including optional detours)
Time: 1 1/3 hours
Public Restrooms: Landmark Center
Note: This walk goes up the stairs of several bridges and down a relatively steep eroded path.

This walk traces the filling of the marshes west of western Back Bay and of the flats in the Charles River west of Gravelly Point (*see map of made land*) that created today's Riverway—an Olmsted-designed park—Park Drive between Riverway and Audubon Circle, Bay State Road—a late nineteenth-/early twentieth-century residential area—and the section of the Esplanade between Charlesgate West and the Boston University Bridge (*see current street map*). The landmaking that filled western Back Bay itself is covered in Walk 7.

1   **Start at the Longwood T station**
Green Line—Riverside ("D") branch.

2   **From the inbound side of the tracks, go down to the walk along the Muddy River. Turn right (upstream) and go to a point just before the Longwood Bridge where the view downstream approximates that in** *1891 and 1892 photos,* a view easier to see when the leaves are off the trees.

1891 photo of the Muddy River downstream from near the Longwood Avenue Bridge

RIVERWAY
The Muddy River was one of two streams that flowed into the western part of Back Bay (*see current street map* for this walk and *1836 map* in Walk 7, p. 110. The other was Stony Brook, which is discussed in Walk 7, ♦ p. 110.) By the late 1870s the Muddy River had become extremely polluted by the sewage discharged into it

1892 photo of the Muddy River downstream from near the Longwood Avenue Bridge

from surrounding sewers. As explained in Walk 7, ♦ p. 110, the Back Bay Fens was created between 1878 and 1894 to deal with the pollution in western Back Bay caused by the sewage brought into it by both the Muddy River and Stony Brook. As part of Back Bay Fens project, the Muddy River was put into a conduit (sewer) from the intersection of Brookline Avenue and Park Drive (*see current street map*) directly to the Charles, bypassing the Fens altogether. But for the part of the Muddy River upstream from (south of) the Fens, Frederick Law Olmsted, the designer of the original Boston parks, had a different plan than the one for Stony Brook, which was put into a conduit and its valley filled. Olmsted suggested that, upriver from the Fens, sewage be diverted from the Muddy River and the waterway left open between artificially constructed banks on which a parkway would be constructed, connecting the Fens and Jamaica Pond. So the winding waterway you see along the first part of this walk is a man-made creation, not the natural wooded stream it appears to be. And the *1891 and 1892 photos looking downstream from near the Longwood Bridge* give you some idea of the grading and filling done to create this effect.

Olmsted first proposed the "Muddy River Improvement," as he called it, in 1880 but the project didn't get underway until 1890. By that time the proposed parkway had been named the Riverway, as it still is, and Olmsted conceived it as one of a series of parkways that would ultimately link the Boston Common to Marine Park in South Boston—what we now call the "Emerald Necklace." In 1890 the boundary between Boston and Brookline (the town on the west side of the Muddy River) was changed so that, even after the river was widened and straightened in accordance with Olmsted's plan, the boundary would still be in the middle of the river. As soon as the boundary was changed Brookline began filling, contracting with the Boston & Albany Railroad to bring gravel fill and then later loam to top it. Boston followed suit on its side of the river in 1891 and by 1893 Riverway was open between Brookline and Huntington Avenues.

Go under the Longwood Bridge and look back at it.   3

The Longwood Avenue Bridge (*photo*), designed by the firm of Shepley, Rutan and Coolidge and completed in 1898, is one of the finest in the Riverway project. It is constructed of seam-faced granite, the seams tinted terracotta, as was the style at the time. (The Boylston Street Bridge in the Back Bay Fens, which you can see on Walk 7, is another example of tinted seams.)

Longwood Avenue Bridge

4   Go up the stairs to the top of the bridge and look at the view upstream. This landscape is also artificially constructed.

5   **Continue across the bridge, cross Longwood Avenue (the street on the bridge), go down the steep eroded path** (not the one immediately next to the bridge but the next one) **to the Boston side of the Muddy River, and start downstream.**
     (The stairs on the Boston side of the Longwood Bridge were omitted as an economy.) As you go downstream, note the embankment that was constructed on the other side of the river to screen the walk from the sight of the tracks, now the Riverside branch of the Green Line (also visible in the *1891 and 1892 photos looking downstream from near the Longwood Bridge*).
     As you approach the Short Street Bridge (the next footbridge over the Muddy River), note that the bridge on the right side of the footpath that seems to arch over nothing actually once spanned a bridle path.

6   **Go out on the Short Street Bridge to approximately the same vantage point from which the *1892 and 1900 photos of Christ's Church, Longwood,* were taken.**

1892 photo of Christ's Church, Longwood

It's difficult to match this view today, because the church is obscured by vegetation even when the leaves are off the trees. But these photographs clearly show the amount of filling and grading done to create what appears to be a natural landscape.

     To see the Round House, an original structure on Riverway, take the short detour below. Otherwise, skip ahead to 7.

6A   Optional detour. At the Short Street Bridge, go up the bridle path bridge (OR just beyond the bridge, go up the bank) to the circular stone rain shelter.

1900 photo of Christ's Church, Longwood

This structure was also designed by Shepley, Rutan and Coolidge. The floor is missing but you can still get a good sense of what the shelter was like. Several more similar shelters were planned further south on the Emerald Necklace but never built.
Return to the walkway along the Muddy River.

From the Short Street Bridge, continue downstream on the walkway. **7**
At the end of the Riverway walk bear left onto Park Drive.
To your right, on the far side of Brookline Avenue between the Fenway and Park Drive, is the Longwood entrance to the Fens (see Walk 7, ♦ p. 111, and *current street map*). The grassy area in front of the Landmark Center, originally built in 1929 as a Sears Roebuck catalog and distribution center—the area bounded by Park Drive, the Fenway, and Brookline Avenue (*see current street map*)—is the fabled "missing link" in the Emerald Necklace. In the 1950s the city sold this area to Sears for a parking lot. It remained an asphalt expanse, breaking the chain of parkland, until 1998 when, after having been returned to the city, it was restored as a park. As you continue up Park Drive, note the red brick Back Bay Yard building on your left, which was built in 1895 as the maintenance facility for the Emerald Necklace.

Cross the tracks (once the Brookline Branch Railroad, now the Riverside **8** Branch of the Green Line) **and go down Park Drive to Audubon Circle (the intersection of Park Drive and Beacon Street). Stop before crossing Beacon Street.**

PARK DRIVE AND AUDUBON CIRCLE
In 1887 when Beacon Street was being widened between Audubon and Cleveland Circles, the Beacon Street residents near Audubon Circle gave the city a one-hundred-foot-wide strip from the circle to the railroad tracks (now the Riverside Branch of the Green Line) so that Beacon Street could be connected to the Fens by a parkway, now Park Drive. This area was marshy and needed to be filled. In 1891 the city contracted with the Boston & Albany Railroad to fill the area with gravel. An iron bridge was constructed over the tracks in 1893 and the filling completed in 1894. Other marshy sections west of present Kenmore Square between the tracks of the Boston & Albany (now the commuter rail next to the turnpike, which is ahead of you) and of the Brookline Branch Railroad (now the Riverside Branch of the Green Line) were filled in the 1880s and 1890s (*see current street map*).

Cross Beacon Street, turn left, take the first right onto St. Mary's Street **9** (the boundary between Boston and Brookline), **cross the bridge over the Mass Pike** (note the railroad tracks next to the turnpike—originally the Boston & Worcester, later the Boston & Albany, and now a commuter line), **cross Commonwealth Avenue, and enter the Boston University campus. Go to the right of Marsh Chapel, take the diagonal brick walkway to the sidewalk, and turn right. At Granby Street this becomes Bay State Road.**

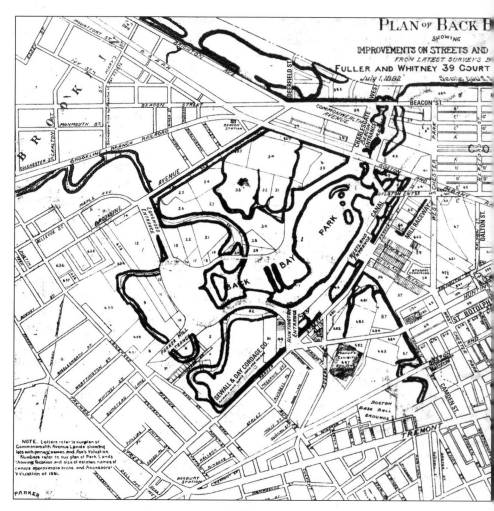

1882 map

BAY STATE ROAD

Bay State Road is on land made in the 1880s and 1890s as a continuation of filling Back Bay. As explained in Walk 6, ♦ p. 101, in 1854 the Boston and Roxbury Mill Corporation (B&RMC) was required to build a seawall two hundred feet north of Beacon Street—at that time a dam called the Mill Dam—and fill the flats between the seawall and the dam from Arlington Street all the way across Back Bay to Kenmore Square. By 1863 the B&RMC had built the seawall and done the filling as far as the cross dam, which intersected the Mill Dam (Beacon Street) between present Hereford Street and Massachusetts Avenue (*see current street map*). But the B&RMC did not begin filling west of the cross dam until 1881 when the Beacon entrance to the Fens was being constructed between present Charlesgate East and West (see Walk

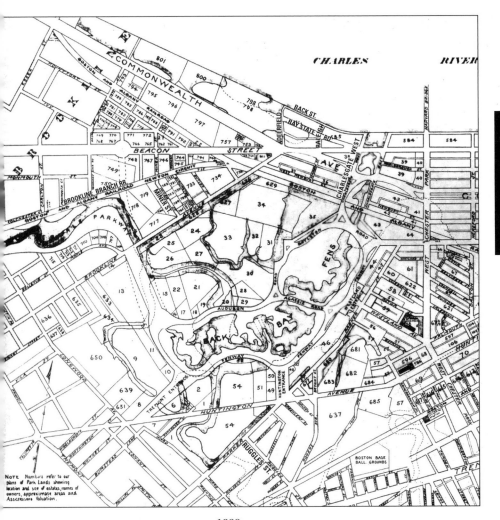

1888 map

7, ♦ p. 111). That year the B&RMC contracted for a continuation of the sea-wall on a line two hundred feet north of and parallel to Beacon Street to a point beyond Charlesgate West, then on a line parallel to what is now Commonwealth Avenue (*see 1882 map*) to Deerfield Street, the western terminus of the B&RMC's flats, and then down the western side of Deerfield Street to what is now Commonwealth Avenue (*see 1882 and current street maps*). Also in 1881 the B&RMC contracted to have the flats inside the seawall filled with material dredged from the river. The filling was completed in 1884 and the seawall in 1886. Then in 1887 the B&RMC filled and graded the streets on the newly made land—Deerfield and Raleigh Streets and the sections of Back Street and Bay State Road between Charlesgate West and Deerfield Street (*see 1888 and current street maps*).

West of Deerfield Street the flats along the river were privately owned by, among others, two grandsons of John Quincy Adams. In 1887 these owners prevailed on the city to widen what had just been renamed Commonwealth Avenue, donating the additional land needed in return for a tax abatement, because they intended to develop their territory north of it as a residential area. In 1889 the Adams brothers, who owned the section between present Deerfield and Sherborn Streets (lot "798" on the *1888 map*; also *see current street map*), contracted to have a seawall built on the outer line of their flats and the flats inside the wall filled with material dredged from the river. That same year the owners of the section between what are now Granby Street and University Road (the connector between Storrow Drive and Commonwealth Avenue just east of the Boston University [B.U.] Bridge)—part of which you've just crossed—also contracted for a seawall and filling of their section (lot "801" and the adjacent lot west of it on the *1888 map*; also *see current street map*).

In 1890 the owners, led by the Adams brothers, formed the Riverbank Improvement Company to develop the whole riverfront between Deerfield Street and what is now University Road. In 1890 they contracted for a seawall and filling of the remaining segment (now the block between Sherborn and Granby Streets—lot "800" on the *1888 map*; also *see current street map*) and by the end of the year the entire seawall from Deerfield Street to present University Road was finished. Most of the filling was completed in 1891, the year the company decided that both Bay State Road and Back Street, the latter a twenty-foot-wide passageway next to the seawall, would be continued across their land (*see current street map*). In 1892 they sold the first lot and within fifteen years Bay State Road was lined with Colonial Revival townhouses that conformed to deed restrictions reminiscent of those for Back Bay: buildings could only be dwellings or outbuildings constructed of brick, stone, or iron; they had to be set back twenty feet from the street; and bowfronts could project no more than five feet.

The town houses and mansions on Bay State Road were originally owned by leading citizens—architects, their clients, and prominent professionals. In the 1920s and 1930s, however, many of the affluent moved to the suburbs and their houses were divided into apartments or doctors' offices. After World War II, when Boston University began to develop its Charles River campus in earnest, the university gradually acquired the Bay State Road houses for dormitories and administrative offices and today owns almost all of the buildings on Bay State Road west of Deerfield Street.

10   **Go down Bay State Road to Sherborn Street.**
This block was originally lot 800 (*see 1888 map*) and was filled by the Riverbank Improvement Company in 1890–1891 (see above). Note the Colonial Revival townhouses, which are typical of Bay State Road.

11   **Turn left on Sherborn Street, cross Back Street** (the narrow alley next to the seawall), **take the footbridge over Storrow Drive, and go to the walk next to the river.**

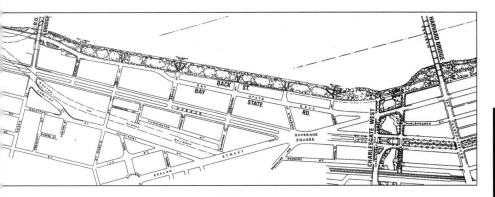

1931 plan

ESPLANADE

From 1890 to the early 1930s the seawall constructed by the B&RMC, private owners, and the Riverbank Improvement Company from Charlesgate West almost to what is now the B.U. Bridge marked the river's edge. In other words, during that period the river was right next to Back Street behind the houses on the north side of Bay State Road. In the early 1930s, however, when the Esplanade east of Charlesgate was being widened (see Walks 4 and 6, ♦ pp. 67 and 104), a 155-foot-wide Esplanade was also filled in front of Bay State Road from Charlesgate West to the Cottage Farm (B.U.) Bridge (*see 1931 plan*). Fill was pumped up from the bottom of the river, through pipes supported by pontoons, and deposited on the shore, causing Bay State Road residents to complain about the continuous "crackling and hissing" noise and the stench of the river bottom mud. The section between Granby Street and what is now the B.U. Bridge was filled with dirt excavated during the extension of the Green Line from Kenmore down both Commonwealth Avenue and Beacon Street (the present "B" and "C" lines). All the fill was sloped down to the water's edge rather than being finished with a seawall in order to reduce the chop formerly created by waves bouncing off a seawall.

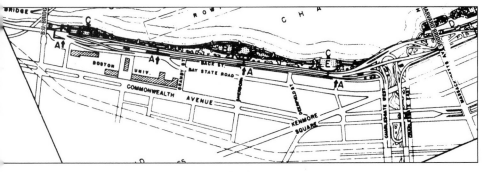

1949 plan

July 31, 1951, photo of hydraulic dredge and Fens gatehouse

As explained in Walk 4, ◆ p. 67, the 1930s Esplanade was created by omitting a proposed highway down the river. That highway, named Storrow Drive, was constructed in 1950–1951, and, in the section between Charlesgate West and the B.U. Bridge, covered most of the Esplanade filled in the 1930s. To compensate for the land taken, an equivalent amount of land was to be created by filling along the river. Plans called for 5.6 new acres with an undulating rather than a straight shoreline in the section between the Harvard (Massachusetts Avenue) Bridge—downriver to your right—and B.U. Bridge—upriver to your left (*see 1949 and 1931 plans*). Much of the fill was dirt trucked in from the suburbs but some was also dredged hydraulically from the river and pumped through pontoon-supported pipes, as it had been in the 1930s (*July 31, 1951, photo.* In this photo note that the Fens gatehouse is on the river's edge.)

12   **Go east (toward the Harvard Bridge) on the Esplanade.**
As you start out, note that you are on land made in 1950–1951 with an undulating shoreline and that the fill slopes down to the water's edge. Also note the 1889–1890 seawall on the far side of Storrow Drive and that the brick buildings on Bay State Road were once almost at the water's edge. As the walk curves under the Storrow Drive on-ramp, note how far inland the Fens

c. 1954 photo of Fens gatehouse and river

gatehouse (the masonry building with a red tile roof visible through the supports of the Storrow Drive overpass—see *photo* in Walk 7, p. 109) is now. More fill was added in front of it in 1954 when Storrow Drive was widened (compare the *July 31, 1951, photo* with a *c. 1954 photo* and the *c. 1966 aerial of Charlesgate* in Walk 7, p. 112).

At the Harvard Bridge, take the footbridge up to Massachusetts Avenue.   13

This is the end of the walk. Nearest T stop—Hynes Convention Center/ICA (Green Line—"B," "C," and "D" branches).

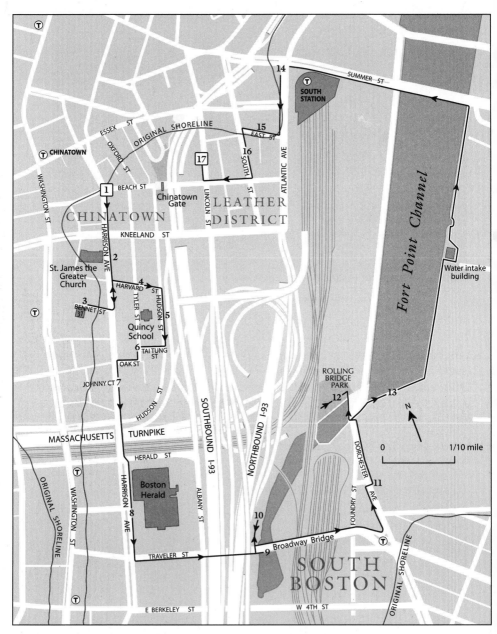

Current street map for Walk 9

Walk 9
SOUTH COVE

Distance: 2 ¹/₂ miles
Time: 1 ³/₄ hours
Public Restrooms: South Station

This walk traces the landmaking in South Cove—the cove originally on the east side of the Boston peninsula formed by Windmill Point on the north and Boston Neck on the west (*see map of made land*). As you can see from the *current street map*, the land made by filling South Cove now comprises the Leather District with its handsome late nineteenth-century buildings, part of Chinatown, the knot of ramps at the intersection of I-93 and the Mass Pike, and, south of the turnpike, the Boston Herald building area. The walk also traces landmaking along the Fort Point Channel, which now forms the eastern boundary of South Cove.

Start at the corner of Harrison Avenue and Beach Street.
Nearest T station—Chinatown (Orange Line).

FRONT STREET PROJECT
Harrison Avenue south of this point is on made land. It was originally called Front Street and was filled as part of a controversy. In 1803, when Boston was growing rapidly, a group of speculators began buying up land on Dorchester Neck (now South Boston— *see map of made land*), intending to develop it as a residential area. The speculators' plan was to annex Dorchester Neck to Boston and to build a bridge from South Street in Boston across South Cove to Dorchester Neck (*see 1797 map*) in order to shorten the land route

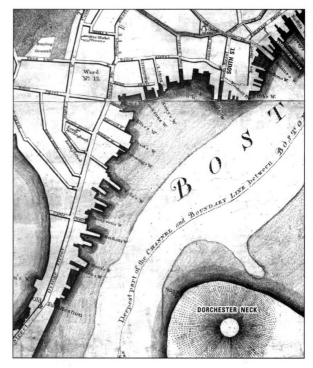

1797 map

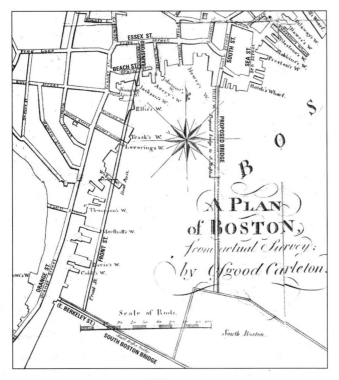

1805 map

between the two, which at the time went all the way around the south end of South Bay (*see made land and current street maps*). But when the speculators proposed this plan to the Boston town meeting in January 1804, it unleashed what one observer called "one of the most violent oppositions that has ever occurred upon a Town question." The opposition came from the wharf owners in South Cove, who claimed that the proposed bridge would cut off their wharves (*see 1797 map*).

The controversy raged until mid-February when, without informing the town or the Dorchester Neck residents, the speculators and the South Cove wharf owners made a deal. The wharf owners, realizing that a bridge was inevitable but wanting it to be in a location least harmful to them, proposed that it be built not from South Street but rather from Orange (now Washington) Street, that is, from the Neck on the line of present East Berkeley Street (*see current street map*). And because this bridge would make the land route to Dorchester Neck much longer than would a bridge from South Street, the wharf owners offered to improve access to the bridge by building a new street to it. This new street, originally called Front Street and now Harrison Avenue, would run from Rainsford's Lane (now the block of Harrison Avenue between Beach and Essex Streets just north of where you are) to the bridge (now East Berkeley Street) parallel to Orange (Washington) Street (*see 1805 and current street maps*).

On March 6, 1804, the legislature passed the three enabling acts: one to annex Dorchester Neck, which was promptly renamed South Boston; another to incorporate the speculators to build the South Boston Bridge; and a third to incorporate the wharf owners as the Front Street Corporation to build the street. Building Front Street obviously meant doing some landmaking (*see*

1805 map). The Front Street project has sometimes been erroneously cited as the "first systematic and co-operative" landmaking project in Boston, but had actually been preceded by the filling in 1794 to create land for ropewalks at the foot of the Common in Back Bay (see Walk 5, ♦ p. 73); in 1800 for the almshouse in the West End (see Walk 3, ♦ p. 46); in 1803 for Charles Street at the foot of Beacon Hill (see Walk 4, ♦ p. 59); and also in 1803 for India Wharf in the central waterfront area (see Walk 1, ♦ p. 14). Construction of Front Street began in May 1804. A seawall was built on the east side of the new street and a fifty-foot-wide road was then filled next to it with mud from flats outside the wall. Front Street was completed in October 1805 as was the South Boston Bridge. The next step of the Front Street project was filling in the flats cut off by the street, which the private owners of these flats did in 1806. Front Street, which was renamed Harrison Avenue in 1841 after the death of President William Henry Harrison, is shown on an *1832 map*.

Note that you are in Boston's Chinatown. Chinese first came to Boston in the 1870s and 1880s, establishing a few laundries on Harrison Avenue and Beach Street, and by 1890 a Chinese community was established in the block north of where you are on Beach Street between Harrison Avenue and Oxford Street (*see current street map*). The Chinese had probably chosen this area because it had low rents and was near a railroad station, and rents were further depressed when an "el" was built on Harrison Avenue and Beach Street in 1901. Until about 1935 Chinatown was located north of Kneeland Street, which is one block south of where you are now, but, after Syrians, who had been living in the area south of Kneeland Street, began moving out and the "el" was taken down in 1942, the Chinese began to move south of Kneeland. This trend was accelerated during World War II when many new Chinese restaurants opened and the immigration laws were changed in 1944, permitting many more Chinese women and families to enter the country. Today, Boston's Chinatown is located on both sides of Kneeland Street between the park over the highway on the east and Washington Street on the west.

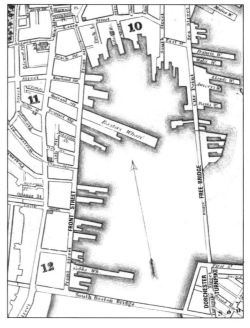

1832 map

2   **Go south on Harrison Avenue.**
At the start, note the Chinatown gate two blocks east on Beach Street and that the corner of Harrison and Beach was at the heart of early Chinatown (see p. 135). As you go down Harrison Avenue note that the original shoreline was to your right (*see current street map*), that Harrison Avenue was originally Front Street, filled in 1804–1806 as explained above, and that between 1806 and the 1830s there would have been land to your right and wharves to your left (*see 1832 map*). The large Catholic church on the right after Kneeland Street—St. James the Greater—was built in 1875 to replace an 1854 church on Albany Street and is a reminder of South Cove's once-large Irish population (see pp. 139–140). If the church is open, go in—it's worth seeing.

3   **Turn right on Bennet Street.**
The house at 37 Bennet Street (*photo*) was built in 1807–1809, just after Front Street was filled, though the house itself is on original land (*see current street map*). In 1859 this house became part of the Boston Dispensary, an outpatient clinic serving immigrants in South Cove, which merged with other institutions in 1930 to become the New England Medical Center.

37 Bennet St.

4   **Return to Harrison Avenue, turn left, turn right on Harvard Street, and cross the next street (Tyler Street).**

SOUTH COVE CORPORATION
In 1804 when the speculators agreed to build the South Boston Bridge on the line of East Berkeley Street (see p. 134), South Boston residents felt betrayed, for such a bridge was not the most direct route between the Boston and South Boston peninsulas. So for many years afterward South Boston residents petitioned for a bridge from South, or later Sea, Street (*see 1805 map*). Finally in 1827 the city permitted a private corporation to build a free bridge (the South Boston Bridge charged tolls) from Sea Street to the Dorchester Turnpike (now Dorchester Avenue) in South Boston. The bridge was completed in 1828 approximately on the line of today's Dorchester Avenue Bridge, which you'll see later on this walk (*see 1832 and current street maps*).

The Free Bridge did make it more difficult for ships to reach wharves in South Cove, just as the wharf owners had predicted, so the owners decided it would be more profitable to fill their flats and develop the resulting land. Thus, in 1833 the South Cove Corporation was formed for the express purpose of filling South Cove to provide land for the terminals of the railroads that were entering Boston at the time. In order to entice railroads, the corporation was authorized to offer a bonus, and the Boston & Worcester Railroad accepted. In 1833 the corporation paid the railroad seventy-five thousand dollars and agreed to sell it land for depots in South Cove.

But first the South Cove Corporation had to make this land. Filling began in May 1833 with mud and gravel excavated at the south end of South Bay and brought to South Cove by scows (*see map of made land map*). Some of the fill was also "cellar earth"—dirt from excavations for new buildings in Boston—and a small amount was gravel from Brighton brought to South Cove by rail—the first time a railroad was used to haul fill in Boston. The corporation had decided to keep the wharves on

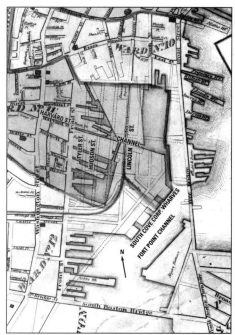

1835 map

Front Street open temporarily, so it left open a channel to these wharves on the line of Harvard Street, where you are now (*see 1835 map*). The corporation had then planned to build a draw-bridge over this channel on the line of Lincoln Street, down which the railroad ran (*see 1835 map*), but when the Boston & Worcester insisted on a fixed bridge instead, which would have prevented masted vessels from reaching the wharves, the corporation decided in 1836 to fill in the wharves after all. Another part of the South Cove project involved building wharves along the Fort Point Channel, the outlet of South Bay. These wharves, in addition to those on the east side of former Sea Street and filling on the South Boston side of the channel, began to define the Fort Point Channel (*see 1838 and current street maps*). By 1839 the South

1838 map

1852 map

Cove Corporation had filled almost all of the cove north of Orange (now Herald) Street (*see 1838 and current street maps*).

♦   The Boston & Worcester soon built depots on the made land (*see 1838 map*) and they were joined in 1845 by the terminals of the Old Colony Railroad, which entered Boston through South Boston (*see 1852 map*). The railroad tracks and depots were located east of Albany Street, while the new land west of Albany was soon built up with brick Greek Revival row houses, many of them occupied by railway workers. Some of these original Greek Revival houses—identified by being three bays (door or window openings) wide with the doorway at one side and by having rectangular lintels over the windows and doors and gabled dormers on the roofs—still remain. You can see them where

Greek Revival houses on Harvard Street

you are on Harvard Street between Tyler and Hudson Streets (*photo*), for example (note that the corner house is shown on the *1852 map*).

Turn right on Hudson Street. 5

Note that the buildings are again original Greek Revival houses (*photo*) and that they are also shown on the *1852 map*. The construction of the Central Artery and Southeast Expressway in the 1950s had a large impact on this area—Albany Street and the buildings on it were removed, leaving the houses on Hudson Street facing a highway retaining wall.

Greek Revival houses on Hudson Street

Go right on Tai Tung Street and cross Tyler 6 Street to the far side.

From the west side of Tyler Street you have a good view of more original Greek Revival houses (*photo*), again shown on the *1852 map*. Just beyond them is the red brick Quincy School, which opened in 1847 and was rebuilt after a fire in 1858. (It is now a Chinese community center.) The Quincy School educated the children of the many different groups that have lived in South Cove. The Greek Revival houses in South Cove were originally occupied by middle-class Americans, but these residents were quickly displaced by the Irish, who poured into Boston after the mid-1840s and settled in South Cove because rents were relatively low owing to the proximity of the railroads. The Irish remained the predominant group

Greek Revival houses on Tyler Street

in South Cove until the 1880s when they began to move out and were replaced by Eastern European Jews and Italians. Neither of those groups remained very long, however, for by 1900 South Cove was predominantly Syrian. The Syrians lived south of Kneeland Street until the 1940s when, as discussed on p. 135, they began to move away and were replaced by the Chinese.

7   **Go south on Tyler Street, right on Oak Street, and left on Harrison Avenue.**
Again, note the original Greek Revival houses on the west side of Harrison Avenue (*photo*) as well as those on Johnny Court (Maple Pl. on the *1852 map*). At the intersection of Harrison Avenue and Hudson Street (on the left just before Harrison crosses the turnpike) note the curve of Hudson, which is reminiscent of the original shape of Curve Street next to the railroad tracks (*see 1838 and 1852 maps*).

Greek Revival houses
on Harrison Avenue

8   **Cross the turnpike on Harrison Avenue.** Note that the commuter rail next to the turnpike is on the alignment of the Boston & Worcester tracks, which now curve to South Station further east than they originally did (see *1852 map and 1901 chart* on p. 142). **Continue down Harrison Avenue.**
The Boston Herald building, on your left, is in an area once known as the "New York Streets." The South Cove Corporation filled this area in the early 1840s (*see 1838 and 1852 maps*) to create residential land. The streets laid out on the new land were named for towns in upstate New York to commemorate the opening of the Western Railroad (an extension of the Boston & Worcester) from Worcester to Albany in 1842—giving the area its name (*see 1852 map*). These streets were soon lined with tenements that were occupied by Irish immigrants, many of whom worked on the railroads. There were still many Irish in the New York Streets at the end of the 1800s, though by that time there were also many Eastern European Jews. The entire New York Streets area was demolished in 1957 as an urban renewal project and the Boston Herald building was then erected in 1959.

◆   Note that Traveler (formerly Troy) Street was the southern end of the New York Streets (*see 1852 map*)—the flats between Troy Street and the South Boston Bridge (now East Berkeley Street, the next light south on Harrison Avenue) were not filled until the late 1860s when Albany Street was extended across this area (see Walk 10, ◆ p. 151).

9   **At Traveler Street, turn left, cross Albany Street** (the section of Albany Street to your right is the part filled in the late 1860s—see Walk 10, ◆ p. 151),

and go out onto the south (right-hand) side of the new Broadway Bridge as far as the first viewing point.

From here you can see the beginning of the Fort Point Channel north of the East Berkeley/West 4th Street Bridge *(photo)*. It's fed by the Roxbury Canal Conduit, which carries the major waterway that flowed out of South Bay (see Walk 10, ◆ p. 157).

Beginning of the Fort Point Channel

◆

Return to the west end of the Broadway Bridge, cross it, and take HarborWalk north next to the Fort Point Channel as far as the fence across the walk. 10

The seawall along the curve in the channel ahead is where the South Cove Corporation's wharves were located.

Retrace your route to the Broadway Bridge, turn left, and go across the bridge to South Boston. At the end of the bridge turn left onto and go up Dorchester Avenue. As you can see on the *current street map*, you are on made land, though landmaking in South Boston is not the focus of this walk. 11

At Foundry Street, cross to the east side of Dorchester Avenue, just before the security booth go back across to the HarborWalk sign, turn right, and go along the Fort Point Channel to Rolling Bridge Park on your left. Enter the park and read the historical panels about the Fort Point channel bridges, Fort Point Channel commerce and Boston landmaking, and the Old Colony Railroad Bridge and South Station. 12

Return down HarborWalk past the security booth, cross the street, and take HarborWalk toward the Gillette building across to and along the South Boston side of the Fort Point Channel. 13

The bridge you see to your left as you start along HarborWalk is the Dorchester Avenue Bridge, approximately on the site of the 1828 Free Bridge to South Boston (see p. 136).

FORT POINT CHANNEL

The Fort Point Channel, along which you are going, is the natural outlet of the two streams that once fed into South Bay—the large tidal bay originally between Boston Neck and South Boston (*see made land, 1797, and current street maps*). These streams are now in covered conduits and discharge into the Fort Point Channel just north of East Berkeley Street, as you saw earlier on the walk. The present configuration of the channel has been defined by filling on both the Boston and South Boston sides, as also noted earlier. As you continue along HarborWalk, the seawall you see on the Boston side of the channel was built as part of the South Station project.

♦ SOUTH STATION

In the mid-1890s the New York, New Haven & Hartford Railroad, which was taking over most of the railroads that entered Boston from the south, agreed to work with the Boston & Albany (the successor to the Boston & Worcester) in building a new union terminal for all the lines entering the city from

♦ the south. The railroads chose a site for the terminal on the Fort Point Channel south of Summer Street, an area that at the time was occupied by wharves (*see 1896 chart*). The seawall that you see was then built along the channel, the wharves filled in, Dorchester Avenue laid out next to the channel behind the seawall, Atlantic Avenue widened, and, as noted earlier on this walk, the tracks of the Boston & Albany moved further east (*see 1896 and 1901 charts*). South Station itself, which you'll see later on the walk, was built on the made land between 1897 and 1899.

When you get to the trellis just before the brick building, stop and read the historical panel about the Gillette Company and the water intake building. On the other side of the water intake building, read the historical panel about the "Big Dig" casting basin, formation of the Fort Point Channel, and commerce along the channel. North of the intake building, the indentation in the side of the channel filled

1896 chart

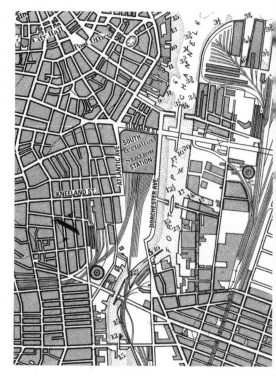

1901 chart

South Station

with rock riprap is the site of a former dock (water in which ships moored, not a structure; *see 1896 and 1901 charts*).

At the end of the walk go straight ahead into the building at the end, go up the stairs, exit onto Summer Street, turn left, and go to the southwest corner of Summer Street and Atlantic Avenue.   14

From here you have a good view of the South Station head house (*photo*). Note that the date on the cornice is 1897, though, as mentioned earlier, the building wasn't completed until 1899.

Go south on Atlantic Avenue and turn right on East Street.   15

Note that the corner of Atlantic and East was once Windmill Point, which defined the northeast edge of South Cove (*see made land and current street maps*). As you go along East Street, you are following the 1630 shoreline (*see current street map*).

Turn left on South Street.   16

South Street is the street from which the bridge to South Boston was originally proposed (see p. 133). This area is known as the Leather District because in the late nineteenth and early twentieth centuries it was the center of the wholesale market for the New England shoe and leather business. Note the handsome 1880s buildings along South Street.

Continue on South Street to Beach Street, turn right, and then right on Lincoln Street.   17

Lincoln Street is where the Boston & Worcester Railroad once ran (*see 1835 and 1838 maps*). On the east (right) side are more handsome late 1800s buildings in the Leather District.

This is the end of the walk. Nearest T stops—about equidistant from South Station (Red Line) and Chinatown (Orange Line).

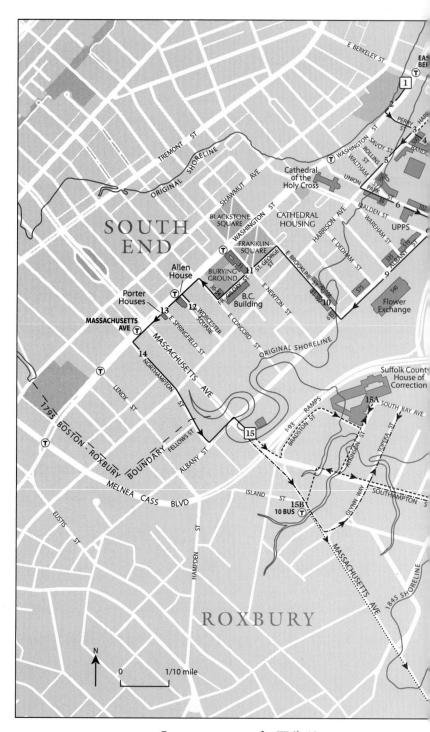

Current street map for Walk 10

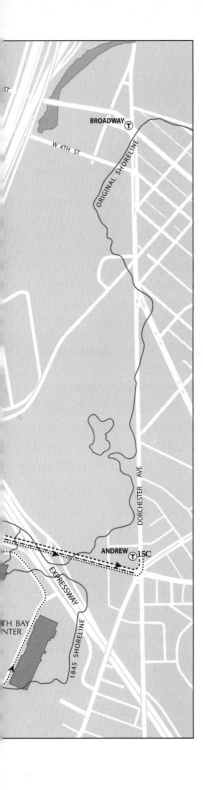

Walk 10
South Bay and South End

Distance: 3 miles (including optional detours)
Time: 1 ²/₃ hours (not including wait for bus)
Note: The optional end of the walk crosses a busy highway.

This walk traces the filling of South Bay, the large tidal bay that once lay between Boston Neck and Dorchester Neck (now South Boston; *see map of made land*). The southern shore of South Bay was originally just north of present Southampton Street, but the bay was enlarged in the 1830s when the South Cove Corporation excavated mud from the south end of the bay to fill South Cove (see Walk 9, ◆ p. 137), creating new flats—later filled—where the South Bay Center is now (*see current street map*). Much of the land made by filling South Bay is now occupied by highways, railroads, and trucking terminals and is not particularly conducive to a walking tour, but some of the landmaking created part of the South End and that is where most of this walk takes place. The walk will take you through a former industrial area in the South End where the factories have been rehabbed for other uses and then through part of the South End on original land. The last part of the walk, which crosses the former South Bay, traces an interesting part of the landmaking story though is not so conducive to walking, as noted above, and so is optional.

1 **Start at the southwest corner of Washington and East Berkeley Streets.**
Nearest T station—East Berkeley Street (Silver Line). On the subway lines, about equidistant from New England Medical Center (Orange Line) and Broadway (Red Line).
Read the "Made Land" historical panel on the back of the Silver Line kiosk. It summarizes most of the landmaking explored on this walk and some of that covered on Walks 5 and 9.

BOSTON NECK
The original Boston peninsula was connected to the mainland by only a narrow neck of land (*see map of made land*) on which there was just one road—a forerunner of today's Washington Street (*see current street map*). East Berkeley Street runs across what was the narrowest part of the Neck, the site of a fortification and the town gates in the 1600s and 1700s. Compare the *1775 view*

1775 view of Boston Neck

of Boston Neck with the view toward East Berkeley Street today. In the *1775 view*, Washington Street (on the right) runs toward the fortification across Boston Neck between Back Bay on the left and South Bay on the right. Boston Neck was low-lying and sometimes awash during large storms, causing colonial Bostonians to be concerned about its erosion. Although most efforts to protect the Neck were made north of the fortification (East Berkeley Street), in 1785 the town granted the flats on either side of the Neck south of the former fortification to a group of proprietors (owners) in return for which they were to drive timber pilings on the west side of the Neck and build a stone seawall on the east (South Bay) side. When the seawall, which extended fourteen hundred feet south from the former fortification—about to present Rollins Street (*see current street map*)—was built, the flats next to it were filled, creating a small amount of new land.

Note that East Berkeley Street is also the site of the bridge built from the Neck to South Boston in 1804 (see Walk 9, ♦ p. 134).

Go south on Washington Street.   2

An elevated train ran down Washington Street from 1901 to 1987, contributing to the deterioration of the neighborhood. Since the mid-1990s there has been a concerted effort to revitalize Washington Street, which is now paying off—you can see some of the new construction, shops, and restaurants before you turn on Perry Street.

Turn left on Perry Street and go to Harrison Avenue.   3

As you go down Perry Street, note that you are crossing the original shoreline of the Neck (*see current street map*).

EXTENSION OF FRONT STREET

The town of Boston originally included not only the Boston peninsula but also the land south of the Neck as far as the 1795 Roxbury boundary (*see current street map*). In 1801, when Boston's population was increasing rapidly, the town decided to develop this land south of the Neck, which was called the Neck Lands. So the selectmen, one of whom was architect Charles Bulfinch, laid out a street grid, and the resulting plan, which was reproduced on an *1814 map*, is reputed to be Bulfinch's design. (Note, by the way, that present Perry and Savoy Streets follow old property lines on the Neck—*compare the 1814 and current street maps.*) People didn't rush to buy the Neck Lands, however—the *1814 map*, for example, shows only a few houses along Washington Street. One reason the Neck Lands were slow to develop is that there was only one road to them—Washington Street. So in 1829 the city decided to extend two new streets to the Neck Lands—Tremont Street on the west side of the Neck and Front Street on the east (*see 1826 and 1835 maps*. The filling that created Tremont Street is discussed in Walk 5, ♦ p. 76.) Most of Front Street (now Harrison Avenue), was laid out on existing, though marshy, land that required building a bulkhead on the east side of the street. But to make the

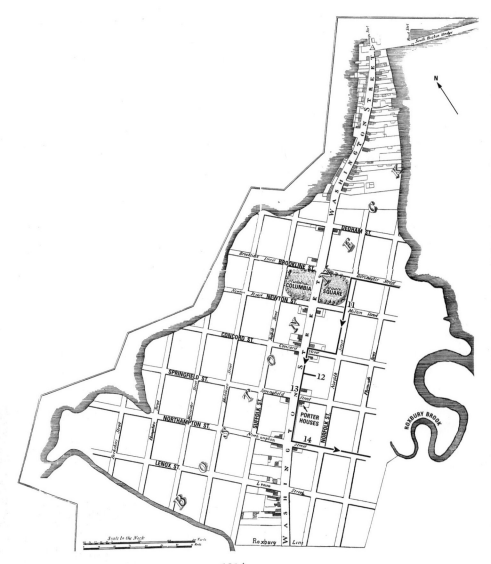

1814 map

section of Front Street between Savoy and East Berkeley Streets, which was a continuation of the Front Street filled in South Cove in 1804–1805 (see Walk 9, ♦ p. 135), a triangle of flats had to be filled (*see 1835 and current streets maps*). This filling was done in 1835–1836, creating the part of Harrison Avenue where you are now.

In the late 1800s this section of Harrison Avenue was an industrial area, and many of the factories still exist, though have been converted to other uses. The building now at 500 Harrison (Bacon's Building), for example, was built in 1875 for a piano manufacturer, one of the major industries in Boston in the late 1800s, with many factories in the South End.

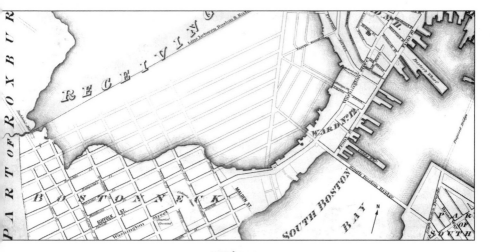

1826 map

Go down the passage to the courtyard of the 500 Harrison building.   4
The huge wheel in the courtyard came from the long building to the north at
460 Harrison Avenue, which was constructed in 1880–1881 to house a variety of manufacturing firms. The center section was the power plant for the
entire building and that is where the wheel was located until moved here in
2003. Also visible in the courtyard is the stack of the Reece Building next
door, which was built in 1895–1896 as a buttonhole machine factory. As you
return up the passageway to Harrison Avenue, note the granite paving blocks
preserved in situ on either side.

To see the SoWa gallery district, take the optional detour below.
Otherwise, skip ahead to 5.

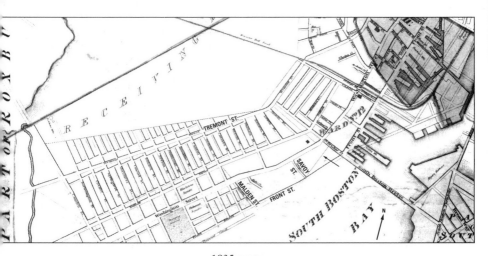

1835 map

4A   Optional detour to the SoWa District. Go north on Harrison Avenue past the 460 Harrison building (Reed's Block) and turn right before the 450 Harrison building (where the overhead banners announce the So-Wa District).

Taking a leaf from New York City, several sections of Boston have recently been dubbed with contracted names—"SoWa" stands for "south of Washington Street" and is an emerging gallery district. The former industrial building at 450 Harrison Avenue, which now houses sixteen galleries along a landscaped walk (open houses 5–9 PM, first Friday of each month), is the heart of this district and a good example of the renovation of this area.

3   Return to the corner of Harrison Avenue and Perry Street.

5   Go south on Harrison Avenue.

As you start down Harrison Avenue, the building on the south corner of Randolph Street was built in 1882 as another piano factory. Savoy Street marks the end of the section of Harrison Avenue filled in 1835–1836 (see p. 148). The large empty building with three gabled bays set back from the east side of Harrison Avenue in the section between Savoy and Rollins Streets was built in 1890–1892 as the power plant for the West End Street Railway, Boston's first electric trolley system. Rollins Street marks the approximate end of the seawall built in the 1780s to protect the Neck (see p. 147). The six-story brick building at 560 Harrison Avenue on the corner of Waltham Street (with "218 Wabash Ave., Chicago" painted on its north side) was built in 1891 as a piano factory. To your right at Union Park Street is the Cathedral of the Holy Cross, built in 1867–1875 to serve the large Irish population then living in the South End.

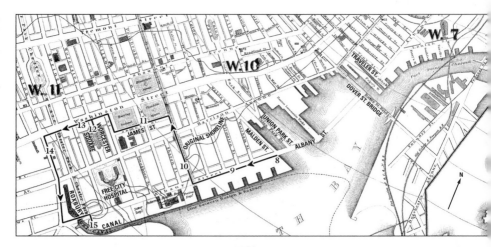

1866 map

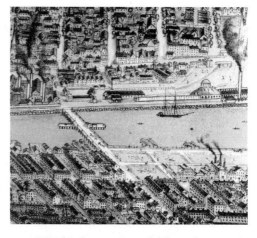

1866 bird's-eye view of Albany Street   1870 bird's-eye view of Albany Street

Turn left on Union Park Street.   6

As you start down Union Park Street, the large brick building on the left is the former piano factory and the one on the right at 89 Union Park was built in the 1890s as a home for working girls. Further down Union Park Street, the early 1900s row houses at 102–134 on the left are one of the few remaining instances in this part of the South End of buildings originally constructed as residences. Across the street from them is the Union Park Pumping ♦ Station (UPPS), first built in 1915 to pump up effluent from low-lying sewers in parts of the South End, particularly in the vicinity of Tremont Street, that had not been filled above the high tide (see Walk 5, ♦ p. 82).

Stop at Albany Street.   7

EXTENSION OF ALBANY STREET   ♦

This section of Albany Street was not filled until the 1860s, later than the section south of Malden Street, which was created in 1845–1862 during the South Bay Lands project discussed on pp. 152–154, or the section north of Traveler (formerly Troy) Street, which was filled in the 1830s and 1840s as part of the South Cove project (see Walk 9, ♦ p. 140). When those two earlier parts of Albany Street were completed, there was a gap between present Malden and Traveler (Troy) Streets (*see 1866 map*) and in the early 1860s the city began to build this missing part of Albany Street. At first just the street itself was constructed by building a seawall across the flats and filling a street next to it. The section of Albany Street between what are now Malden and East Berkeley Streets (the latter formerly the South Boston, or Dover Street, Bridge), where you are now, was completed in 1864 (*see 1866 map*), and you can see it south of the bridge on a detail from an *1866 bird's-eye view*—note that the flats between the street and the shore are still open. The section of Albany Street north of the ♦ bridge—between present East Berkeley and Traveler Streets—was constructed in 1866. After the street was finished, the flats between the street and shore were filled. This filling was completed about 1870, as you can see on an *1870 bird's-eye view*, which shows the newly filled flats between Albany Street and Harrison Avenue (compare it with the *1866 view*). So, as you were going down Union Park Street, you were crossing the flats filled in the late 1860s during what was called the extension of Albany Street project.

8   **Turn right on Albany Street, go to the corner of Malden Street, and cross to the east side of Albany.**

SOUTH BAY LANDS

♦   In the mid-1840s, when Irish immigrants fleeing the potato famine in Ireland were pouring into Boston, the city was anxious to keep middle-class Yankees, who were valued both as taxpayers and as voters who could counter the Irish, from moving to the suburbs by providing attractive residential areas for them within the city. The only existing area available for such development, however, was the South End—the former Neck Lands—which was still

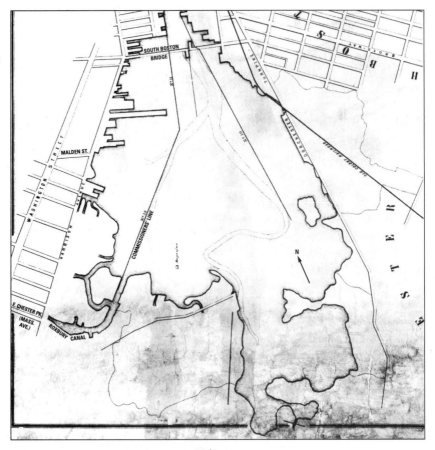

1845 map

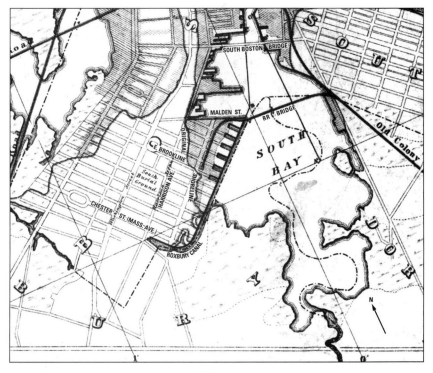

1852 map

very sparsely populated despite the extension of Tremont and Front Streets in the 1830s (see p. 147). So, in the 1840s the city graded streets, planted trees, and built sewers in the South End. These sewers created a potential problem, however, for at this time Boston sewers discharged raw sewage at the nearest shoreline. Realizing that sewage emptying onto the flats in South Bay next to Harrison Avenue would detract from the planned residential area, the city decided to fill these flats and extend the sewers out to deeper water in South Bay. Thus, in 1845 the city initiated what was called the South Bay Lands project to fill the area now bounded by Malden Street, Harrison and Massachusetts Avenues, and the I-93 ramps (*see 1845 and current street maps*).

The plan was to build a seawall approximately on the commissioners' line shown on an *1845 map*, fill the intervening flats, and also create six wharves between Malden and East Brookline Streets, as shown on an *1852 map*. (Note the *1852 map* also shows the original shoreline of Boston as well as the filling done by 1852—indicated by gray shading—so clearly shows the amount of land that would be created by the South Bay Lands project. Also note that the original shoreline is indicated on the *1866 map*.) Initially the fill was gravel brought by the Old Colony Railroad from Quincy and then across South Bay on a bridge constructed especially for the project (*see 1852 map*). To carry out the work, the city had the misfortune to contract with a William Evans, who turned out to be one of the most litigious and difficult contractors with whom the city dealt in the mid-1800s. Evans invariably sued for damages on any contract the city made with him, and his claims were so exorbitant that the city always felt obliged to make a new contract in order to settle the claims against the previous one. Matters came to a head on the South Bay Lands project in 1858 when one of the wharves Evans had built collapsed in a storm and another was seriously damaged—and then Evans won one of the contracts to repair his own deficient work! Evans finally completed the South Bay Lands project in 1862, having created about sixty-seven acres of new land.

9　**Continue down Albany Street.**

The land made by the South Bay Lands project did not become the middle-class residential area the city had intended. The section of Albany Street that you are going down became industrial, as you can see. The large building at 519 Albany, in the block between Malden and Wareham Streets, for example, was built in two sections as a piano factory—the north half in 1902 and the south half in 1887. The building at 535 Albany, on the south corner of Wareham Street, was built in 1888 as a planing mill. The Flower Exchange, at 540 Albany Street on the east side of the street, is where the wharves on South Bay were once located (*see 1866 and current street maps*). (If you want to visit the exchange, it's open weekdays 5 AM–noon, Saturdays 6–10 AM. Go in any entrance off Albany Street and check in at the glassed-in office in the center.) Returning to Albany Street, the building at 575 on the southwest corner of East Dedham Street was originally a lumber and planing mill and the building at 615 Albany Street (Naval Blood Research Laboratory), on the south corner of East Brookline Street, was built in the 1860s as a factory to manufacture cases for organs. South of East Brookline Street the land between Albany Street and South Bay became the location of many city departments—paving, internal health, sewer, and water (*see 1866 map*).

10　**Turn right on East Brookline Street.**

As you go up East Brookline Street, note that the houses at 107–81 on the left and 108–70 on the right are typical South End brick row houses with bow fronts and cast iron railings—one of the few parts of the South Bay Lands that did develop residentially. On your right at Harrison Avenue the yellow brick buildings are Cathedral Housing, a public housing project built in 1948–1952 in an area formerly occupied by older row houses.

11　**Turn left on St. George Street.**

Neck Lands

The next part of the walk is on original land in the South End and is included to get you from the part of South Bay filled by the South Bay Lands project to the part filled in the twentieth century. This section of the walk looks at some of the remaining features from the 1801 plan for the Neck Lands (*see 1814 map*). St. George Street itself, for example, is the surviving remnant of

Norfolk Street. (Suffolk Street, on the other side of Washington, still exists as Shawmut Avenue. And the cross streets from Dedham to Lenox shown on the 1814 map are also still there, though usually interspersed with additional streets—see current street map.) The park on the west side of St. George Street between East Brookline and East Newton Streets is now Franklin Square. It is actually half of Columbia Square laid out in 1801 (see 1814 map; the other half, Blackstone Square, is on the other side of Washington Street) and was landscaped in the 1860s when the South End was being developed. The large building at 11 East Newton Street ("The Franklin") was built in 1868 as the St. James Hotel. In 1882 it became the New England Conservatory of Music and then, when the Conservatory moved in 1901 to its present location on Huntington Avenue (see Walk 7, ◆ p. 115), a nonprofit hotel for working women called the Franklin Square House. It has now been converted into apartments for senior citizens. Although not on the 1814 map, the burying ground in the block after East Newton Street was established in 1810 as a potter's field (a burial ground for paupers, unknowns, and criminals). It is esti-

mated that about 11,000 persons are buried here, most of them members of the working class in graves with no headstones. For more information, see the green plaque on the Washington Street side. The large building on the east side of St. George Street (this part now named Fr. Gilday Street) between East Newton and East Concord Streets (photo) is one of the original buildings of Boston College. The center section was constructed between 1858 and 1860 closer to Harrison Avenue (it's

Original Boston College building

the upper part of the U-shaped building near James Street on the 1866 map) and moved back sixty feet to James (now Fr. Gilday) Street in 1874. At that time the building was extended to connect it with the Immaculate Conception Church (now the Jesuit Urban Center) on Harrison Avenue, and both ends of the building were extended again in 1889–1890. In 1913, when Boston College moved to Chestnut Hill, Boston College High School, which had been in the same building but with a different curriculum since the 1890s, became the building's sole occupant and remained so until 1950, when B. C. High moved to its present location on Morrissey Boulevard in Dorchester. The building is now being converted into luxury condominiums.

Turn right on East Concord Street, noting the building at 30–34 East   12
Concord, which was built in the early 1870s as a carriage factory (note the large doorways). **Turn left on Washington Street.**

c. 1865 photo of Boston City Hospital from Worcester Square

At the corner of Washington Street and Worcester Square, read the green plaque on the Allen House on the south corner. **Turn left into Worcester Square.** Compare the present view (best seen when the leaves are off the trees) with the *c. 1865 photo of Boston City Hospital* from the same vantage point. The hospital is on land between Harrison Avenue and Albany Street at the south end of the South Bay Lands project, which became devoted to institutions, particularly hospitals, rather than residences. Boston City was built in 1862–1864 (*see 1866 map*; note that the building shown in the *c. 1865 photo* no longer exists). Boston City was soon joined in that area by the Massachusetts Homeopathic Hospital and the Children's Home and is today the Boston Medical Center.

13 **Return to Washington Street, turn left, and go to the northeast corner of East Springfield Street.**
On the southeast corner of Washington and East Springfield are the Porter Houses (*photo*), back-to-back Federal-style houses that are the only buildings shown on the *1814 map* still in existence.

14 **Continue down Washington Street and turn left on Northampton Street.**

Porter Houses

NORTHAMPTON STREET DISTRICT
Northampton Street was the northern boundary of an area known as the Northampton Street District—the area bounded by Northampton, Washington, Eustis, and Albany Streets (*see current street map*)—which, although not originally tidal flats, was very marshy and so low-lying that sewers couldn't drain at high tide. To correct this, in 1874 the city raised the entire ground level of this district by adding fill on top of the existing surface, jacking up the houses and other buildings in order to do so, just as the city had done a few years earlier in the Church (Bay Village) and Suffolk (Castle Square/Mass Pike Towers) Street Districts (see Walk 5, ♦ pp. 75–76 and 77).

So as you go down Northampton Street, note that the area to your right is the one that was raised.

Continue down Northampton Street (Boston's notorious mayor James Michael   15
Curley was born in 1874 at no. 28 Northampton Street, which was on the right
just before Fellows Street), **turn left on Albany Street, go to Massachusetts
Avenue and cross it, turn right, and go to the parking lot just beyond the
five-story brick building set back from the street on the left.**

ROXBURY CANAL
The Roxbury Canal was the outlet of former Roxbury Brook, one of two   ◆
streams that fed into South Bay and one that had been contained in a channel in the early 1800s (*see 1814, 1845, 1852, and 1866 maps*). The canal
served the wharves behind Albany Street, as you can see on an *1896 chart* on
p. 158, and even when most of South Bay was filled in the first half of the
1900s, the canal and the channel behind the Albany Street wharves were
dredged so that shipping could still use them (see p. 160 and *1911 and 1934
charts* on p. 159). By the late 1920s, however, the part of South Bay that still
remained open had become extremely polluted; a 1929 report complained of
the offensive odor, particularly in the Roxbury Canal. But nothing was done
then or even when the Southeast Expressway was built across South Bay in
1956–1959, filling most of the bay but leaving the Roxbury Canal still open,
as you can see in a *1950s aerial photo*. (In this photo, Massachusetts Avenue
runs diagonally across the lower right corner and is intersected by Albany
Street, which is parallel to the canal. You can see the same five-story brick

1950s aerial photo of Roxbury Canal

building you have just passed and that the canal ran just behind it. In other words, you are now on the site of the canal.) Building the expressway actually increased pollution in the Roxbury Canal, for it had pushed up bottom mud, which, saturated with sewage, decaying organic matter, and fuel oil, emanated "foul odors that permeate the atmosphere for a mile or more," according to a 1958 report. The report went on to say that the appearance of the canal was "revolting" and that it was an "open cesspool," particularly serious because it ran right behind Boston City Hospital. Using capital letters for emphasis, the report recommended that the Roxbury Canal be filled "AS SOON AS POSSIBLE." But *still* nothing was done until finally, in 1965–1966, the state put the Roxbury Canal into an underground conduit and filled its former channel behind Albany Street. (The Roxbury Canal Conduit now discharges into the Fort Point Channel just north of the East Berkeley/West 4th Streets Bridge—see Walk 9, ♦ p. 141.)

This is the end of the main part of the walk. Nearest T station—Massachusetts Avenue (Silver Line). To trace the filling of South Bay in the twentieth century, take the optional end of the walk below. This part of the walk can also be covered by car, if one is available. Driving directions are included at the end of the walking directions.

15A Cross the I-93/I-90 entrance ramps—be careful (note the Roundhouse Suites building to the right ahead—it's a converted nineteenth-century holder for manufactured coal gas) and turn left on Bradston Street. Go up the street, turn right at the end and go past the Suffolk County House of Correction on the left, at the end turn left on Atkinson Street, and go to the corner of Atkinson and South Bay Avenue. If driving, heading southeast on Massachusetts Avenue starting opposite stop #15, cross the I-93/I-90 entrance ramps (note the Roundhouse Suites in a converted holder for manufactured coal gas on the right) and take the left fork (marked I-93 and 3) to Southampton Street. Go straight across Southampton to Topeka Street (no street sign) and down it to South Bay Avenue at the end (no street sign).

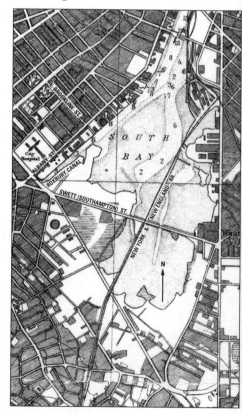

1896 chart

FILLING THE REST OF SOUTH BAY

In the 1890s a large part of South Bay was still open (*see 1896 chart*). During that decade it was suggested that the material dredged from the Roxbury Canal (see p. 157) be used to fill parts of South Bay that were no longer navigable. The idea received impetus in the late 1890s when South Station was built over wharves on the Fort Point Channel (see Walk 9, ♦ p. 142), creating a demand for more wharves in South Bay. So, between 1902 and 1907 the area between Southampton Street and a line extended from East Brookline Street was filled, new wharves were built at the south end

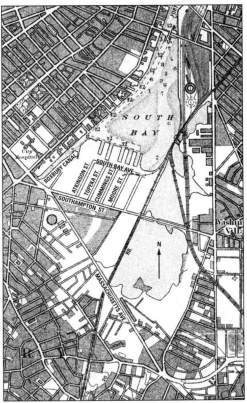

1911 chart

of South Bay, and new streets were laid out from Southampton Street to these wharves (*see 1911 chart*). Where you are now—the intersection of Atkinson Street and South Bay Avenue if you walked and Topeka Street and South Bay Avenue if you drove—was at the head of one of these wharves (*see 1911 chart*).

Soon after these wharves were completed, people became concerned about pollution in South Bay. Although Boston had built a sewerage system in the mid-1880s, the sewers carried both sanitary wastes and storm water and often overflowed during large storms, carrying sewage

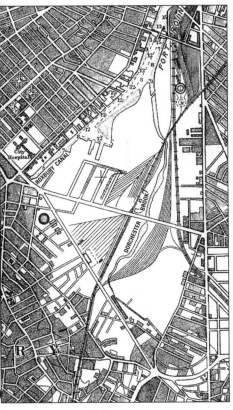

1934 chart

W
A
L
K

10

into bodies of water like South Bay. A board set up in 1914 to investigate pollution in South Bay found that, in addition to sewage, the east side of the bay was becoming choked with trash and next to the Fort Point Channel the bay was "offensive to the eye at all seasons and malodorous to the nose in warm weather." Nonetheless, the board equivocated and in the end did not recommend filling the bay.

Perhaps because this attempt to fill South Bay had failed, in 1920 when the New York, New Haven & Hartford Railroad requested permission to fill most of the bay for rail yards, a license was readily granted. By 1929 the railroad had filled all of the bay except the Roxbury Canal (see p. 157), the channel serving the Albany Street wharves, a turning basin at the south end that served the wharves there, and Dorchester Brook, the other stream that flowed into South Bay (*see 1934 chart*). In the 1950s, when the Southeast Expressway was constructed across South Bay, the turning basin was filled. In 1957 the city then constructed a huge incinerator on the made land north of where you are now on South Bay Avenue where the wharves had formerly been located, and the incinerator's three tall stacks dominated the skyline when leaving the city on the expressway (*photo*) until 1998, when the incinerator was torn down. (The photo was taken looking north on the expressway toward the

Cathedral of the Holy Cross in the South End, which you saw earlier on this walk, with the incinerator at the left. And the jail you passed when walking was built in 1990, even before the incinerator was demolished, to replace an antiquated facility on Deer Island.) The part of South Bay that remained open north of the turning basin as well as Dorchester Brook and the Roxbury Canal were not filled until 1965–1966 after the canal and brook had been put into underground conduits (see p. 158).

1969 photo of the Southeast Expressway and South Bay incinerator

15B Return down Atkinson Street and continue past Bradston Street to Southampton Street. Turn right on Southampton, cut left through the gas station/McDonald's parking lot, cross Massachusetts Avenue to the Island Street bus stop, and take the #10 bus to the Andrew T station.

OR, at the end of Atkinson Street turn left on Southampton Street and walk to the Andrew T station. OR, if driving, return down Topeka Street to Southampton Street and turn left.

Southampton (originally Swett) Street was built across South Bay in the mid-1870s to provide a direct route between Roxbury and South Boston (*see 1896 chart*), a project that required a small amount of landmaking.

If you take the bus, you will go through the South Bay Center, which is in the part of South Bay that was enlarged in the 1830s when the South Cove Corporation dug mud there to fill South Cove (*see current street map* and Walk 9, ♦ p. 137), excavating the existing tidal marsh below the high tide line and thus changing it into tidal flats. This part of South Bay was filled in the early 1920s by the New York, New Haven & Hartford Railroad, as explained above. If you walk or drive, note the South Bay Center to your right as you go up the bridge to cross the Southeast Expressway—the present size of the center approximates the area excavated in the 1830s.

Andrew Square or T station (Red Line) is the terminus of the optional end of   **15C** the walk.

W
A
L
K

10

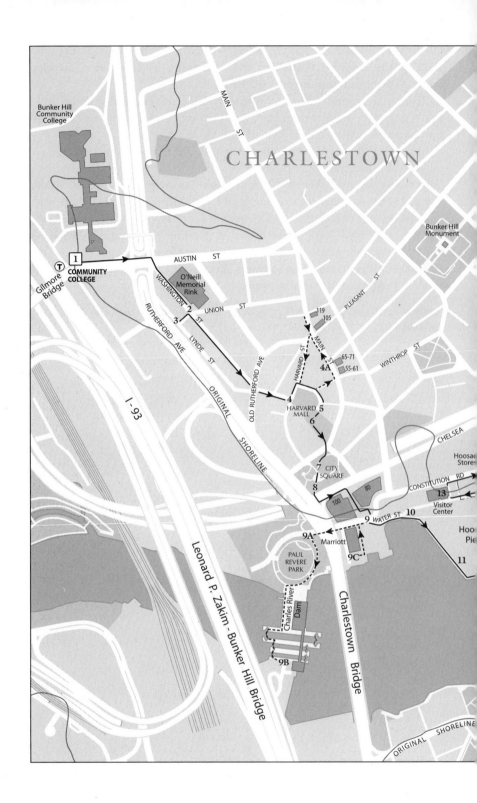

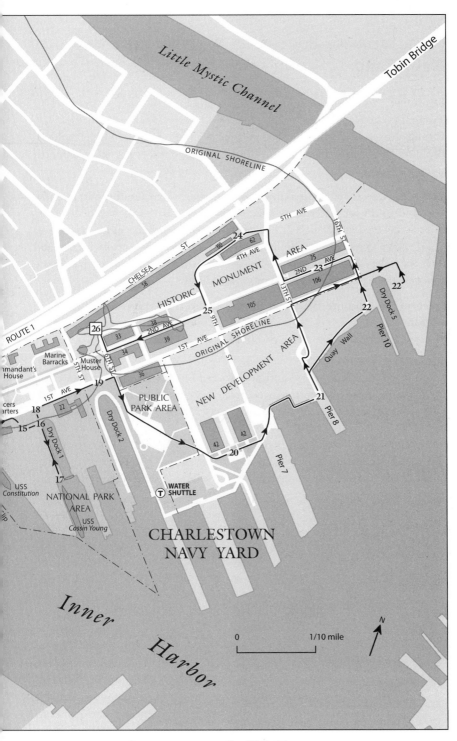

Little Mystic Channel

Tobin Bridge

ORIGINAL SHORELINE

5TH AVE

16TH ST

CHELSEA ST

58

4TH AVE

60

24

62

HISTORIC

MONUMENT AREA

75

2ND AVE

23

106

13TH ST

105

25

ROUTE 1

26

2ND AVE

38

9TH ST

1ST AVE

ORIGINAL SHORELINE

22

Dry Dock 5

Pier 10

Quay Wall

22

Marine
Barracks

Muster
House

33

34

39

36

NEW DEVELOPMENT AREA

ST

Commandant's
House

5TH ST

19

8TH ST

PUBLIC
PARK AREA

21

Pier 8

Officers
Quarters

1ST AVE

18

22

Dry Dock 2

42

42

20

Pier 7

15—16

Dry Dock 1

17

WATER
SHUTTLE

USS
Constitution

NATIONAL PARK
AREA

USS
Cassin Young

CHARLESTOWN
NAVY YARD

Inner

Harbor

0   1/10 mile

N

Current street map for Walk 11

Walk 11

CHARLESTOWN—SOUTHWEST WATERFRONT AND NAVY YARD

Distance: 3 4/5 miles (including optional detours)
Time: 2 3/4 hours
Public Restrooms: Navy Yard Visitor Center (Bunker Hill Pavilion), Building 5, Constitution Museum (Building 22), outdoor pay toilet on north side of Dry Dock 2

This walk traces the landmaking that has occurred on Charlestown's southwest and southeast waterfronts—landmaking on Charlestown's north waterfront is covered in Walk 12. The walk will explore the oldest section of Charlestown with its late eighteenth- and nineteenth-century houses and then trace the landmaking in the Navy Yard, which has numerous handsome and well-preserved nineteenth-century buildings.

1   **Start on the Gilmore Bridge at the exit from the Community College T station.**
Nearest T station—Community College (Orange Line).

SOUTHWEST WATERFRONT
Like Boston, Charlestown was originally a peninsula connected to the rest of the mainland only by a narrow neck (*see map of made land*), but it was founded in 1629, a year earlier, by another group of Massachusetts Bay colonists. In the 1600s and 1700s Charlestown was an important port and manufacturing center, and some developments mirrored those in Boston. Charlestown also had a mill pond, for example, having dammed off the head of the inlet between the Charlestown peninsula and what later became Somerville (*see key map*) about 1645 in

1993 reconstructed drawing of Charlestown mill dam and mill in 1805.

order to power tide mills (*see 1775 map*; see Walk 2, ♦ p. 32, for a discussion of Boston's 1640s tide mill project). You can't see the location of the mill dam or mills from here— they were to your left beyond Bunker Hill Community College near the present Hoods Milk stack—

1775 map

but a *1993 reconstructed drawing*, which shows the mill dam and mills in the foreground, gives a sense of what they looked like.

Charlestown's 1700s prosperity came to an abrupt end on June 17, 1775, during the Battle of Bunker Hill (actually fought on Breed's Hill, which was mislabeled on the *1775 map*) when British ships firing from Boston and the river (represented by the long dotted lines on the *1775 map*) set Charlestown on fire and it burned to the ground. Reconstruction began in the 1780s and by the early 1800s Charlestown had almost completely recovered.

In 1800 Massachusetts decided to locate the new state prison in Charlestown, purchasing land and flats on a point on Charlestown's southwest shore. The state then evidently filled and squared off the shoreline of what was henceforth known as Prison Point (compare *1818 and 1775 maps*), and the new prison, designed by architect Charles Bulfinch, opened in 1805. Bunker Hill Community College, to your left, is on the site of the prison, which was demolished in 1957.

The Gilmore Bridge, where you are now, is on the site of the Prison Point Bridge, built in 1815 to connect Charlestown and East Cambridge (*see 1818 map*). Actually, the Prison Point Bridge was built as an arm off of another bridge—Craigie's, which had been constructed in 1809 to connect Lechmere Point (East Cambridge) with Boston's West End (*see 1818 map*).

The Prison Point Bridge was the first of many bridges across Prison Point Bay, as the tidal inlet between Charlestown and what is now Somerville became known. Most of these bridges were built for the numerous railroads that crossed Prison Point en route to Boston (*see 1848 and 1879 maps*) and by the late 1860s they so obstructed the tidal flow in the bay that it had become a "nuisance"—an obnoxious smell, sight, or obstruction. Proposals then began to be made to fill the bay, which the state finally ordered done in the early 1880s "for the preservation of the public health." The made land in

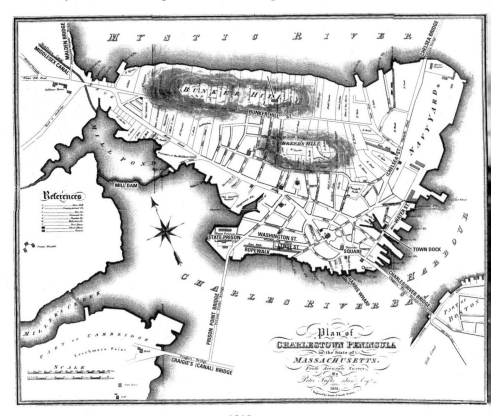

1818 map

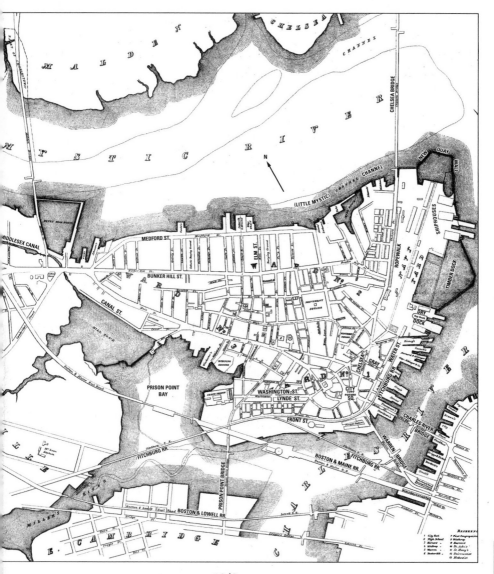

1848 map

Prison Point Bay then became a vast rail yard for the Boston & Maine Railroad. The rail yards were removed in the 1960s, however. The southern part of the former yards became the athletic fields of the community college and the northern part, near the Hoods Milk plant, are now occupied by a recycling center and other light industries.

Go down the Gilmore Bridge (toward the Bunker Hill Monument), 2 cross Rutherford Avenue and Austin Street (the continuation of the bridge), go up the steps or ramp on the right just before the O'Neill Memorial Rink, and go down Washington Street (no street sign).

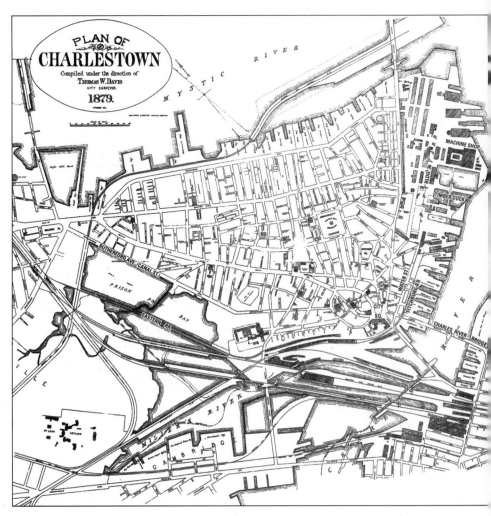

1879 map

As you can see on the *1818 map*, Washington Street was once very near the shore. It was developed in the early 1800s—the row of brick Greek Revival houses on your right was built in 1839, for example.

3 **At Edward L. Johnson Square (the end of the first block), turn right on Union Street (no street sign) and go down to Lynde Street (the alley-like street behind the houses on Washington Street).**
In the early 1800s Lynde Street was almost at the water's edge and a ropewalk ran next to it (*see 1818 map*). In 1836 the Charlestown Wharf Company was incorporated to develop the waterfront between the Prison Point Bridge and the Navy Yard, that is, the section where you are now (*see 1818 map*). The company's plans were tied to a new railroad, the Charlestown Branch Railroad, also chartered in 1836 to provide a connection between the Boston

& Lowell Railroad, which had entered Boston in 1835 (see Walk 2, ♦ p. 37) from East Cambridge, and the deepwater wharves on Charlestown's southeast waterfront next to the Navy Yard. The railroad built a spur track from the Boston & Lowell in what is now Somerville across Prison Point Bay to Prison Point. Then the wharf company built a seawall between the Prison Point and Warren Bridges and filled behind it, creating new land for the railroad tracks and a new street next to them named, appropriately, Front Street, which was in front of where you are now (*see 1848 map*).

In 1843 the Fitchburg Railroad, a new line entering Boston from the north, acquired the Charlestown Branch Railroad as well as the land the Charlestown Wharf Company had made. The Fitchburg did some additional filling and in 1848 built a bridge across the Charles to its new depot on Causeway Street in Boston (see Walk 2, ♦ p. 42). Meanwhile, in 1845 the Boston & Maine, yet another railroad entering Boston from the north, built its tracks across Prison Point and filled an island in the river for a roundhouse and other facilities. All these developments are depicted on an *1848 map* of Charlestown, which shows, in comparison with the *1818 map*, the amount of new land that had been made. Now, Rutherford Avenue (in front of you) runs where Front Street once did and I-93 (the elevated highway) is in the vicinity of the former Fitchburg and Boston & Maine tracks.

In the second half of the 1800s, railroad bridges continued to be built across this area, especially after the Eastern Railroad changed its route in 1854 to enter Boston from Charlestown instead of from East Boston. By the 1870s Prison Point Bay and the Charles River were choked with railroad bridges (*see 1879 map*), obstructing the tidal flow in Prison Point Bay and leading to its filling, as discussed on p. 166.

Return up Union Street, turn right on Washington Street, cross Old Rutherford Avenue (note the nice view to the right of the Zakim Bridge), **and continue to Harvard Street at the top of the hill.**   4

CHARLESTOWN IN THE 1600S AND 1700S
When Charlestown was founded in 1629, an engineer sent with the colonists to lay out the town devised the street plan shown on the *1775 map*. The streets encircled Town Hill, one of the town's high points, and when Charlestown was rebuilt after the Revolution (see p. 165), this street plan informed the new one (*see 1818 map*), though Town Hill was reportedly cut down somewhat. At the top of Town Hill is the Harvard Mall; the houses around it were built in the 1800s.

To see some of the houses constructed when Charlestown was rebuilt after the Revolution, take the optional detour below. Otherwise, skip ahead to 5.

Optional detour to see late eighteenth-century houses. Go left around the Harvard Mall and down Hurd's Lane (the stone-paved narrow street that heads toward a large granite church with brick trim) to Main Street.   4A

On the northeast (right) side of Main Street from Winthrop to just beyond Pleasant Street are a number of notable examples of houses built in the late 1700s (best viewed from the west side of Main Street): the Deacon Larkin House (c. 1795) at 55–61 Main (*photo*), the John Hurd House (c. 1795) next to it at 65–71 Main, the Warren Tavern (c. 1780) at 105 Main (corner of Pleasant), and the Timothy Thompson Sr. House (c. 1794) at 119 Main at the corner

Deacon Larkin House

of Thompson Street. These houses may have survived because between 1901 and 1975 an elevated train ran down Main Street between City and Sullivan Squares, discouraging development on Main Street.

Retrace your route on Main Street, bear right at the stone house (1822) onto Harvard Street, and go up Harvard Street to the Harvard Mall.

5   **From Harvard Street, go left around the Harvard Mall.**
Note the early 1800s houses, including a small stone house, on the left side just before an entrance to the Mall.

6   **Enter the Harvard Mall.**
Read the historical plaques on the walls and the incised inscriptions at the base of the flagpole. They have information about the original settlement of Charlestown and about John Harvard, an early settler of the town who, when he died in 1638, left a bequest and half his library to the new college the colony had founded in Cambridge, which was then named for him.

7   **Go down the steps, cross Main Street at the bottom, and enter the park in City Square.**
Charlestown has had an open square in the location of present City Square throughout its history (*see 1818, 1848, and 1879 maps*). The square was once the location of an open air market and, in the second half of the 1800s, of Charlestown's City Hall. (Charlestown adopted a city form of government in 1847 and remained a separate city until it was annexed by Boston in 1874.) For most of the 1900s City Square was adversely affected by transportation facilities—an elevated train ran across it from 1901 to 1975 and an overhead highway after the mid-1950s. But the el was taken down soon after it closed in 1975, the highway has now been put into a tunnel under the square, and the square itself has been rejuvenated as a park.

Read the historical markers, one on the history of City Square from Native American occupation through the twentieth century and the other on the Great House/Three Cranes Tavern archaeological site, which was excavated as part of the "Big Dig." The Great House was built in 1629 for John Winthrop, governor of the Massachusetts Bay Colony, in anticipation of his arrival in

1630. Winthrop only resided in Charlestown for a few months, however, before moving across the river to Boston in the fall of 1630. In 1635 the Great House became a tavern, later named the Three Cranes, and remained one until it was burned on June 17, 1775, during the Battle of Bunker Hill. The outline of the tavern is marked with stones in the ground.

Go to the south corner of City Square, at the corner of Chelsea Street and Rutherford Avenue. (Note another spectacular view of the Zakim Bridge.)   **8**

CHARLES RIVER AND WARREN BRIDGES

From this point you can see the bridge going across the Charles River (marked by the overhead green route signs) to the main part of Boston. This bridge, known as the Charlestown Bridge, is approximately on the site of the very first bridge that connected the original Boston peninsula and the mainland. Constructed in 1785–1786 and known as the Charles River Bridge (*see 1818 map*), it replaced a ferry on the same spot. The income from this ferry had been granted to Harvard College in 1640, a grant that was still in effect in the 1780s, so, to compensate Harvard for the loss of revenue, the proprietors of the Charles River Bridge were required to pay Harvard £200 a year. Then, in 1823 residents of Charlestown proposed building another bridge across the Charles. Named the Warren Bridge, it would be free, in contrast to the Charles River Bridge, which charged tolls, and would be on almost the same route. The proprietors of the Charles River Bridge objected vigorously, but the legislature finally approved the Warren Bridge in 1828 and it was constructed that same year (*see 1848 map*). The controversy did not end there, however. The proprietors of the Charles River Bridge sued, but they lost twice in the state Supreme Judicial Court, and, in a famous case, in 1837 they also lost an appeal to the U.S. Supreme Court.

The Warren Bridge remained in use until 1954, when it was replaced by a new bridge of the Central Artery. The discontinued Warren Bridge burned in 1962 and at about that time was chosen as the site for the new Charles River Dam (the red brick building you can see between the Charlestown and Zakim Bridges; see p. 172).

Cross Chelsea Street, turn left, turn right through the arch between the 100 and 80 City Square buildings, and go down the steps on the left to the street at the bottom. To see the new Charles River Dam, take the optional, and highly recommended, detour below. Otherwise, skip ahead to the resumption of 9, below.   **9**

Optional detour to the new Charles River Dam. From the foot of the steps, turn right and go under the Charlestown Bridge to Paul Revere Park.   **9A**

On the wall at the entrance to the park, note Revere's account of his famous ride on April 18, 1775, to warn the countryside that the British were coming to seize a store of arms in Concord.

WALK 11

NEW CHARLES RIVER DAM

In August 1955 Hurricane Diane dumped so much rain into the Charles River Basin that it rose four and a half feet above normal. The water could not flow out through the Charles River Dam fast enough and at high tide could not flow at all. As a result, surrounding areas flooded, particularly some low-lying parts of Cambridge, causing millions of dollars in damage. To avoid similar floods in the future, a pumping station was recommended but, since there was not room for such a station on the old dam (where the Museum of Science is located), it was decided to build a new dam. The site eventually chosen was the old Warren Bridge (see p. 171), and the new dam—the brick building in front of you—which is essentially a huge pumping station, was constructed between 1974 and 1978. In the process a small amount of new land was made between the dam and the Charlestown Bridge (*see current street map*).

9B   Go left around the park and go up the steps of the dam building to see the nine bronze panels on the wall, which depict the history of the Charles River. Then go to the right of the dam building and follow the walkway next to the river to the three sets of locks.

The locks through the dam mark the demarcation between the fresh water of the Charles River (on your right) and the salt water of the harbor (on your left). If you're lucky, you'll see a boat going through the locks. **Retrace your route and go back under the bridge to the steps of the 80 City Square building.**

9   **At the foot of the steps of the 80 City Square building.**

SOUTHEAST WATERFRONT

Water Street, the street ahead of you next to the parking lot, was for many years the main street across Charlestown's southeast waterfront (*see 1775, 1818, 1848, and 1879 maps*). Until the 1830s it crossed the mouth of the Town Dock (*see 1775 and 1818 maps*), an enclosed anchorage that had been excavated in the late 1600s on the site of a natural inlet (*see current street map*). (Note that until the last century, the term "dock" meant the *water* into which a ship sailed, *not* a structure to which it moored.) In the 1600s the first dry dock in North America was constructed in what became the center arm of the Town Dock, probably by lining the sides and bottom of the arm with planks and constructing a gate at the harbor end. Unlike Boston, where enclosed docks were filled in the 1700s (see Walk 1, ♦ pp. 6, 10, and 21), Charlestown's Town Dock remained open and active into the early 1800s—archaeological investigations in the 1980s found remains of an early 1800s seawall and wharves in the dock, probably built to serve a large rum distillery on the dock's northeast side. But by the 1830s the Town Dock had become quite polluted and was filled in. Gray Street, which no longer exists, was then laid out right down the middle of the former dock (*compare 1848 and 1818 maps*).

After the Town Dock was filled in, wharves continued to be built on Charlestown's southeast waterfront, among them the wharf of Frederic Tudor, who made a fortune shipping ice cut from Boston-area ponds to the South, the Caribbean, and India. Tudor Wharf is now the location of the Marriott Residence Inn.

For a short optional detour to read some historical markers, go around the Marriott (on your right) to the wharf in front of it. 9C
Read the historical displays about Charlestown's waterfront, immigration, and Tudor's ice trade.
Return to the steps of the 80 City Square building.

Continuing at the steps of the 80 City Square building. 9
The wharves on Charlestown's southeast waterfront were served by the Fitchburg Railroad, as you can see on the *1848 and 1879 maps*, and in the late 1880s the railroad developed these wharves into a major shipping terminal. Named the Hoosac Docks after the tunnel under Hoosac Mountain in the Berkshires whose completion in 1875 had provided the Fitchburg with a direct rail connection between Boston and the West, one of these large wharves, or piers, still remains.

Go to the walkway along the water next to Water Street (to the left of the parking lot), turn left, and go to the HarborWalk sign on your right. 10
Note that the area extending from where you are on Water Street to beyond Chelsea Street was approximately the location of the Town Dock (*see current street and 1818 maps*).

Take HarborWalk around Hoosac Pier. 11
This very large pier is what remains from the Fitchburg Railroad's Hoosac Docks development in the late 1880s and early 1890s (see above and *1896 chart* in Walk 12, p. 189). As you start out, there is a good view of the Charlestown Bridge to your right. After you round the northeast corner of the pier you have a great view of the *Constitution* ("Old Ironsides"), built in 1797 and now the oldest commissioned ship in the U.S. Navy. The body of water in which the ship is moored is called the Fitchburg Slip (*photo*), created by the railroad in 1899 partly on navy property. Note that the sides of the slip are formed by steel sheet piling—often used in landmaking projects in the 1900s in place of the stone seawalls of the 1800s. Also note the large brick Fitchburg warehouse, known as Hoosac Stores Nos. 1 and 2, at the end of the slip and the freight cars in front of it—both reminders that this was once a shipping pier served by railroads. Finally, note the angled end wall of the three-story red brick building with a hip roof (Building 5) behind the *Constitution* in the Navy Yard, a wall built on the original boundary of the yard.

Fitchburg Slip

12 **At the end of HarborWalk around the Hoosac Pier, turn right (in front of the boxcars) and go to the Paul Revere Landing Site.**

This is the place where Revere landed after he'd rowed across the river from Boston on April 18, 1775, in order to begin his famous ride. You can read the historical plaques to find out more.

13 **Retrace your route to the end of Hoosac Pier and follow the Freedom Trail red line on Water Street to the Charlestown Navy Yard Visitor Center (the Bunker Hill Pavilion).**

Go into the center, get the Charlestown Navy Yard brochure, which has a useful map and information, and, if you wish, watch the Battle of Bunker Hill film (a twenty-minute presentation every thirty minutes on the half hour from 9:30 to 4:30; Bunker Hill is visited on Walk 12).

14 **Exit onto Constitution Road, turn right, and enter the Navy Yard through Gate 1.**

Just before you enter the Navy Yard, note the ivy-covered granite and brick wall to your left, which lines up with the original end of red brick Building 5 on your right and marks the original boundary of the yard.

NAVY YARD

The Charlestown Navy Yard was founded in 1800, making it almost as old as the U.S. Navy itself. The navy was established in 1794 when Congress authorized six frigates built to protect American ships from pirates off the North African coast. One of these frigates, the *Constitution*, was built in a private shipyard in Boston's North End and, as mentioned above, launched in 1797. But when Congress appropriated money for more ships in 1799, the new secretary of the navy thought that this time they should be built in navy shipyards. So in 1800–1801 six navy yards were established, one of them in the Boston area. (The others were in Portsmouth, N.H., Brooklyn, N.Y., Philadelphia, Washington, D.C., and Norfolk, Va.) The site chosen for the Boston navy yard was actually in Charlestown—35$\frac{1}{2}$ acres on the southeast waterfront stretching from north of the Town Dock to Moulton's Point at the northeast tip of the peninsula (*see 1775 and 1818 maps*).

The original shoreline of the Navy Yard ran approximately along today's 1st Avenue, where you are now (*see current street map*), and the navy soon began to fill the flats fronting the yard for various projects. Building 5, for example, the three-story red brick building on the right that you also saw from across the Fitchburg Slip, was built in 1813 as a storehouse and is at least partially on made land (*see current street map*).

15 **Go down 1st Avenue and turn right at the end of Building 5.**

You are now on land made in the 1800s for various navy yard wharves. To your right is "Old Ironsides," whose construction is related to the founding of the Navy Yard (see above. If you want to visit the ship, tours are every half hour on the half hour 10:00–3:30 Tuesday–Sunday, April 1–October 31 [ship open

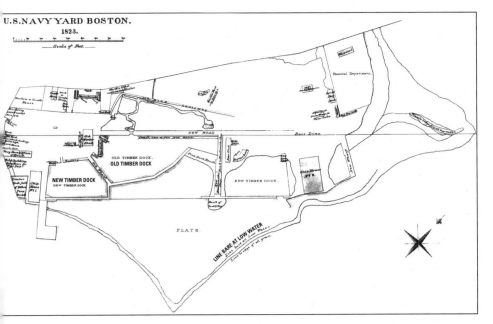

1823 map

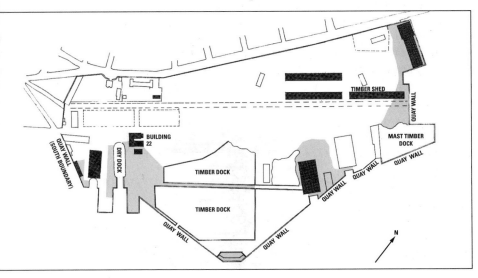

1834 map

10–5:50], Thursday–Sunday, November 1–March 31 [ship open 10–3:50]; closed Mondays). To your left is Dry Dock 1, constructed in 1827–1833 on the site of a former timber dock (see *1823 and 1834 maps;* on the latter map, areas filled since the last map in the series, in this case the 1823 map, are shown in gray). Timber docks were enclosures on the waterfront where shipbuilding timber was stored in seawater, because in the early 1800s it was believed that salt water hardened wood and destroyed harmful acids in it.

16 **Go to the head of Dry Dock 1.**

Dry Dock 1 was constructed by driving a foundation of over four thousand wooden pilings into the underlying clay on the flats and then building stepped walls of granite blocks that had been brought from a quarry in Quincy, Massachusetts (just south of Boston), by an early horse-drawn railroad as far as the Neponset River and then by barge to Charlestown. The former timber dock was then filled in around these walls (*see 1834 map*). Dry Dock 1 opened on June 24, 1833, when the *Constitution*, whose long-planned overhaul had been delayed so that she could inaugurate the dock, entered amidst much ceremony. And it was probably at this time that the commemorative inscription that you see at the head of the dock was chiseled—"Commenced 10th July 1827. John Q. Adams, President of the United States. Samuel L. Shepard, Secretary of the Navy. Authorized by the Nineteenth Congress. Opened 24th June 1833. Andrew Jackson, President of the United States. Levi Woodbury, Secretary of the Navy. Loammi Baldwin, Engineer." Once a ship had entered the dry dock, the entrance was sealed by a caisson (*photo*), a vessel-shaped gate that fitted into grooves and was installed by filling it with water and sinking it into place and removed by pumping out the water and floating it away. After the caisson was in place, water was removed from the dock by steam-powered pumps. The pumps were housed in Building 22, built in 1832, also partly on made land (*see 1834 map*), and now the Constitution Museum (open daily 9–6 May 1–October 15; 10–5 October 15–May 1; free but donation requested).

Dry Dock 1 caisson

17 **Go down to the harbor end of the dry dock (toward the *USS Cassin Young*) to view the caisson.**

Dry Dock 1 is not only the oldest dry dock at the Navy Yard but also the only one still in use. The *Nobska*, the ship now in it, is the last tall stack coastal steamship in the United States (see the historical display at the head of the dock).

If you wish, visit the *USS Cassin Young*, typical of the thirty-six destroyers built at the Charlestown Navy Yard during World War II. Although not built in Charlestown, the *Cassin Young* was serviced here in the 1950s. (Open daily July 1–August 31, 10–5, guided tours at 11, 1, 2, 3, 4; September 1–November 30 and April 1–June 30, 10–4, guided tours at 11, 2, 3; open December 1–March 31, Monday–Wednesday for guided tours only at 11, 2, 3, Thursday–Sunday 11–3, guided tours at 11, 2.)

Return up the side of Dry Dock 1 to 1st Avenue. 18

On the other side of 1st Avenue, note some of the early buildings on original land at the Navy Yard—the Officers' Quarters (1833), Commandant's House (1805; the double bowfront facade reputedly being the result of the architect's having asked the commandant what design he wanted for the house and the commandant's having replied, "My arse!"), and the Marine Barracks (1811, but completely altered; *see current street map*). For more information about aspects of the Navy Yard that will be covered later on this walk, read the historical markers—"Serving the Fleet" (next to the large horizontal wood mast on the southeast side of 1st Avenue), "The Changing Yard," "The Yard as Home," and "Working in the Yard" (on the northwest side of 1st Avenue, the last one near the Scale House).

Go around Building 22 (Constitution Museum) to Dry Dock 2. 19

Dry Dock 2 was built between 1899 and 1906 as one of four new navy dry docks constructed to accommodate a new class of battleship built in the 1890s. (Ironically, just as Dry Dock 2 was being finished in 1906, the British launched

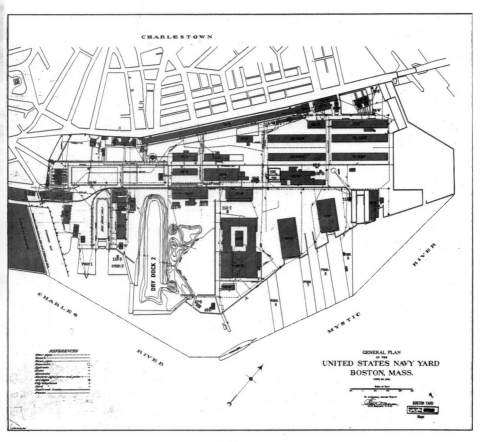

1901 map

a much larger type of battleship, making Dry Dock 2 obsolete even when it opened.) In the early 1830s the navy had built a stone seawall, termed a "quay wall," around the outer line of flats at the Navy Yard, using the areas then enclosed as timber docks (*see 1848 map*). Dry Dock 2 was built in the southern part of what remained of the timber dock in the center of the yard (*see 1879 and 1901 maps*) and, as part of the project, the rest of that dock was filled in.

20   **Leaving Dry Dock 2 on your right, go diagonally through the Public Park area.** Note the long granite Building 36 on your left, which was built in 1866 as a joiners shop and paint loft partly on land made by filling in the central timber dock (*see 1848 and 1879 maps*). Visit the Korean War memorial, if you wish. **Go to the end of Steam Engineering Building No. 42, the large purplish brick building with a slate hip roof and huge arched windows.**

In the 1850s when the navy was finally beginning to build steam-powered ships, it constructed a large machine shop complex at the Navy Yard to service these ships. The machine shop, which was originally a U-shaped complex with a smoke stack even taller than the Bunker Hill Monument, was built on land made by filling in the north part of the central timber dock (*see 1848 and 1879 maps*).

When the Navy Yard closed in 1974, the former yard was divided into four areas—the National Park, where you began; the Public Park area, which you have just crossed; the New Development area, where you are now, which was slated for residential development; and the Historic Monument area (*see current street map*). The former machine shop, which is in the New Development area, has now been converted into residences, as you can see.

21   **Continue along the water toward the north end of the Navy Yard.**
Note the new condominiums on Pier 7 (Constellation Wharf) and, in front of the town houses near Pier 8, remains of two shipbuilding ways (wood ramps on which ships were constructed; *photo*). From the north side of Pier 8 there is a good view of the remaining part of the 1830s quay wall.

Shipbuilding ways

22   **If HarborWalk along the quay wall north of Pier 8 is not yet open, go up 13th Street (at the end of Pier 8), turn right on 1st Avenue** (Building 106 [The Basilica] on your left was built in 1904 as the metalworkers shop; it is now residences and was named The Basilica by the developers), **cross 16th Street (at the end of Building 106), continue straight, turn right into a parking lot surrounded by a chain-link fence, and immediately turn right to the head of Dry Dock 5. OR, if HarborWalk north of Pier 8 is open, take the walk to Dry Dock 5.**

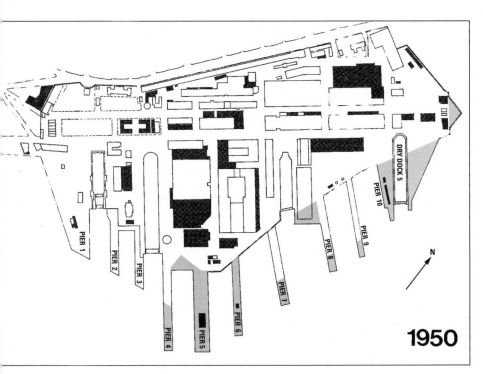

1950 map

Dry Dock 5 was built very hastily in 1942 as a facility in which to construct some of the 300 ships built at the Navy Yard during World War II. As you can see, the sides of the dock are formed by steel sheet piling. One side of Dry Dock 5 was formed by Pier 10 and the other by the land made after steel sheet piling was driven around the northern end of the yard, creating the present pointed shoreline—the last major landmaking at the Navy Yard (*see current street and 1901 and 1950 maps*).

If you are on the north side of Dry Dock 5, retrace your route. The large overhead bridge ahead of you is the Tobin Bridge, which is approximately on the site of the Chelsea Bridge, first built across the Mystic River in 1803 (*see 1818 map*). **Turn right on 16th Street and left on 2nd Avenue. OR, if you are on the south side of Dry Dock 5, go up 16th Street** (see above comment on Tobin Bridge) **and turn left on 2nd Avenue.**

The next part of this walk is primarily on original, rather than made, land at the Navy Yard. Its purpose is to return to the water shuttle to Long Wharf, the recommended end of the walk. This section of the walk goes through the Historic Monument area (*see current street map*), where the exteriors of buildings must be preserved but the interiors can be renovated for office or research use, and includes some of the important early buildings in the yard.

As you go down 2nd Avenue, Building 75 on your right was originally a timber shed built in 1831. Not all the navy's timber was stored in timber docks (see p. 175) in the 1800s—some was also stored in sheds like this one. The shed was originally a series of granite posts with large wooden doors (the present shutters) rather than sides. The northern end of the building is on land made when the quay wall was built around this end of the yard (*see 1834 map*).

24 **Turn right on 13th Street (at the end of the timber shed), cross 4th Avenue, and turn left after Building 62 (the granite building on the left).**

Building 62 was the Hemp House (*photo*), built in 1837 to store hemp fibers for the Navy Yard's famous ropewalk. A ropewalk was a very long narrow structure in which rope was made by workers walking backward, twisting the hemp fibers into rope. The great innovation of the Navy Yard ropewalk was the use of steam-powered spinning and twisting machines, replacing hand labor. Behind the Hemp House

Hemp House

is the ropewalk itself, Building 58, also completed in 1837. The Navy Yard's ropewalk is a quarter of a mile long, allowing the production of rope up to 1,200 feet in length, and made all the navy's cordage until the mid-1950s. Go up close to the ropewalk for a view down its entire length (it originally extended even beyond where you can see cars crossing in the distance). Further down is Building 60, the Tar House (1837). After a length of rope was completed it was dipped into a vat of hot tar to waterproof it. Hot tar was flammable and a danger to ropewalks (wooden ropewalks often burned), which is undoubtedly why at the Navy Yard the tar was in a separate building and the ropewalk itself is of stone.

25 **Go between the brick addition to the Hemp House and the Tar House to 4th Avenue, turn left on 9th Street, and right on 2nd Avenue.**

Building 105, on the north side of 9th Street, was built in 1903 and became the yard's anchor chain forge. Besides the ropewalk, the other industrial innovation for which the Charlestown yard was noted was the invention in 1926 of dielock chain, a steel anchor chain formed by joining two U-shaped links. The Charlestown Navy Yard produced most of the anchor chain for navy ships built during World War II, and in the 1960s it was the only yard manufacturing the huge chain used by aircraft carriers.

As you go down 2nd Avenue, Building 39 on your left was built in 1866 as an ordnance storehouse, Building 38 on the right in 1854 as a packing house and cooperage, Building 34 on the left in 1837 as a storehouse, and Building 33 on the right in 1850 as a cordage storehouse. The octagonal building on the right after you cross 6th Street (at the end of Buildings 33 and 34) was built in 1853 as the Muster House, where employees gathered each morning to receive work assignments.

Turn right on 5th Street and go up to the ropewalk.   26

From here you can have another view down the entire length of the ropewalk (*photo*).

Ropewalk

End of walk. Nearest T station—water shuttle to Long Wharf, which leaves from the pier on the north side (left-hand side as you face the harbor) of Dry Dock 2. This boat trip is highly recommended, for it gives you a wonderful view of Boston's waterfront. At Long Wharf, the nearest T subway station is Aquarium (Blue Line).

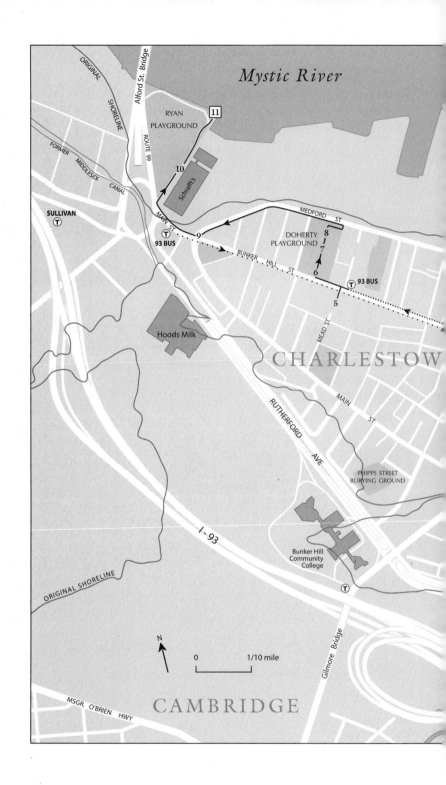

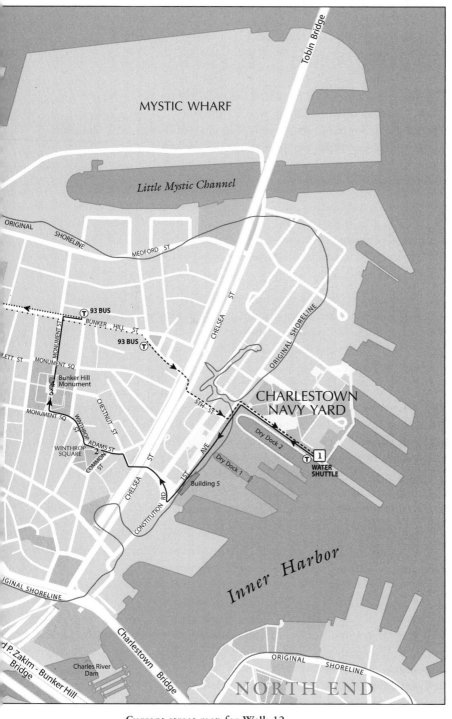

MYSTIC WHARF

Little Mystic Channel

ORIGINAL SHORELINE

MEDFORD ST

Tobin Bridge

CHELSEA ST

ORIGINAL SHORELINE

93 BUS

BUNKER HILL ST

93 BUS

LETT ST

MONUMENT ST

MONUMENT SQ.

Bunker Hill Monument

MONUMENT SQ.

CHESTNUT ST

5TH ST

CHARLESTOWN
NAVY YARD

Dry Dock 2

WINTHROP ADAMS ST

WINTHROP
SQUARE

COMMON ST

1ST AVE

Dry Dock 1

WATER
SHUTTLE

CHELSEA ST

Building 5

CONSTITUTION RD

IGINAL SHORELINE

Inner Harbor

Charlestown Bridge

d P. Zakim - Bunker Hill
Bridge

Charles River
Dam

ORIGINAL SHORELINE

NORTH END

Current street map for Walk 12

Walk 12

CHARLESTOWN—BUNKER HILL MONUMENT AND NORTH WATERFRONT

Distance: 1 3/4 miles (not including bus routes or alternate end of walk)
Time: 1 1/2 hours (not including wait for bus)
Public Restrooms: Constitution Museum (Building 22), Building 5, Bunker Hill Monument, pay toilet on north side of Dry Dock 2
Note: This walk goes up some moderate hills and up and down the 294 steps of the Bunker Hill Monument.

This walk is a continuation of Walk 11. If you continue straight from Walk 11, you can take the water shuttle at the end of this walk rather than at the beginning. The main feature of this walk is the climb up Bunker Hill Monument to view landmaking projects on all of Charlestown's waterfronts. The walk also visits a historic section of Charlestown and several parks.

1 **Start at the water shuttle landing on the pier next to Dry Dock 2.**
The water shuttle, which leaves from Long Wharf in Boston—nearest T subway station is Aquarium (Blue Line)—is not only the T stop closest to the beginning of this walk but is also highly recommended for its wonderful views of the Boston waterfront.

2 **From the landing, go up next to Dry Dock 2 and turn left on 1st Avenue. Exit from the Navy Yard through Gate 1, turn right on Constitution Road, and cross Chelsea Street. Following the Freedom Trail red line, go through the viaduct under the highway, up Chestnut Street, and bear left on Adams Street to Winthrop Square.**
The square was originally named the Training Field and much of the fighting during the Battle of Bunker Hill occurred here. Note the early buildings, particularly the Salem Turnpike Hotel (1795 and 1805) at 16 Common Street and the Federal-style house (1806) at 14 Common Street.

3 **Continue up the Freedom Trail (Adams Street, Winthrop Street, and Monument Square) to the Bunker Hill Monument.**
Between Winthrop and Monument Squares, you have been going through a section of Charlestown developed primarily in the mid-1800s, with most of the houses built for prominent Yankee residents of the city. But many of the Irish who poured into Boston after 1845, fleeing the potato famine in Ireland, settled in Charlestown, and by 1865 22 percent of Charlestown was foreign-born, three-quarters of them Irish. Large numbers of Irish continued to settle in Charlestown and by 1910 Irish comprised 90 percent of the population. Charlestown has remained primarily Irish-American, though there are now a number of young professionals attracted by Charlestown's well-preserved historic houses.

The Bunker Hill Monument marks the Revolutionary battle fought on June 17, 1775, on *Breed's* Hill—the battle was subsequently mistakenly named for the wrong hill in Charlestown because of errors such as the reversed labels on the *1775 map* in Walk 11, p. 165.

Climb the Bunker Hill Monument.   4

If it is a clear day, the climb up 294 steps to the top of the monument is well worth it, for only from there can you get a good view of major landmaking projects on the north and southwest sides of Charlestown. (Open 9–5 daily except Thanksgiving, Christmas, and New Year's; last start time up the monument is 4:30. Fifteen-minute ranger talks are given at the base of the monument daily at 10, 11, 12, 2, 3, and 4.)

From the top of the Bunker Hill Monument, compare the *1848 view north from the Bunker Hill Monument*, which is part of a 360° panoramic view, with the present view north (from the window next to the metal steps). You can see the Tobin Bridge on the site of the former Chelsea Bridge in the *1848 view north* and get a sense of the amount of made land (the original shoreline was approximately on Medford Street, which runs between the closer housing project of red brick and the further one with dark brown siding.)

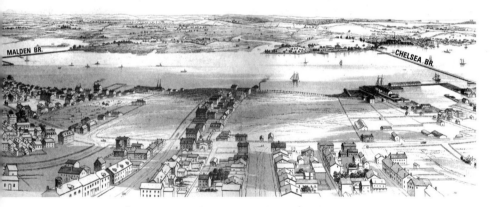

1848 view north from the Bunker Hill Monument

MYSTIC WHARF

The huge wharf separated from the further housing project by a channel is Mystic Wharf (*see current street map*). The Mystic Wharf project had its inception in the 1850s. Charlestown owners of property on the Mystic River east of Elm Street wanted to fill the flats in front of their holdings but were prevented from doing so by the existence there of a navigable channel, which by law could not be filled (*see 1848 map* in Walk 11, p. 167). To overcome this obstacle, these owners combined with the shoreline owners west of Elm Street (the street now next to the brown eight-story buildings at the west end of Mystic Wharf) and got permission to fill a large expanse of flats in the river (the sperm whale–shaped area enclosed by a dotted line where the word "River" is written on the *1848 map* in Walk 11, p. 167) for the benefit of all the owners, who were incorporated in 1852 as the Mystic River Corporation. In 1859 the corporation began building a seawall on the north side of the channel that separated the flats from the shore—now called the Little Mystic Channel (*see current street map*)—filling some flats behind it, and in the 1870s the Boston & Lowell Railroad built a railroad track out onto the prospective wharf (*see 1879 map* in Walk 11, p. 168). But relatively little was done to complete the project until the Boston & Maine Railroad acquired all the flats in 1887. The railroad then pursued the project vigorously, building a seawall on the north side of the flats along the main channel in the Mystic and creating a new dock west of the Chelsea Bridge. In 1889 the Boston & Maine built a timber bulkhead on the line of Elm Street to close off the west end of the wharf and by 1891 had finished the filling (*see 1896 chart,* p. 189). The railroad then constructed a large grain elevator, freight warehouses, and coal pockets on Mystic Wharf, creating one of the major shipping terminals in the harbor. Today only the part on the east side of the Tobin Bridge is called Mystic Wharf; the main part is known as the Moran terminal and is the Boston pier for imported cars. And the Little Mystic Channel, the navigable channel between the wharf and the shore, must still remain open, as you can see.

At the far left from this window you can see the Alford Street Bridge, which is on the line of the former Malden Bridge in the *1848 view north.*

Moving to the next window left, you can see the area shown in the *1848 view west from the Bunker Hill Monument,* another section of the panoramic view— Bartlett Street (to the right of the Charlestown High School building) goes toward the neck (now Sullivan Square), the Hood plant (with the stack) is approximately where the mill pond once was, the athletic fields of Bunker Hill Community College are on the site of former Prison Point Bay, and the college itself is on the site of the state prison. In both the 1848 and present views, note the Phipps Street Burying Ground, established in 1630 at the water's edge. The

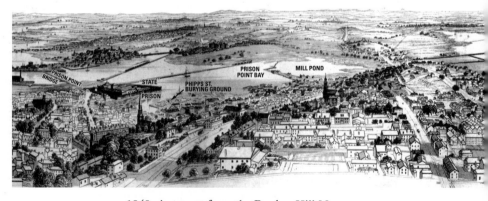

1848 view west from the Bunker Hill Monument

Gilmore Bridge (the street on the right of the Quonset-roofed hockey rink) is on the site of the Prison Point Bridge (see *1848 view west*).

The view from the next window left is approximately the same as that in the *1848 view south from the Bunker Hill Monument* (line up the dome of the State House in both the 1848 and present views). You can see the steel-truss Charlestown Bridge on the site of the Charles River Bridge, the new Charles River Dam (a red brick building) on the site of the former Warren Bridge, the

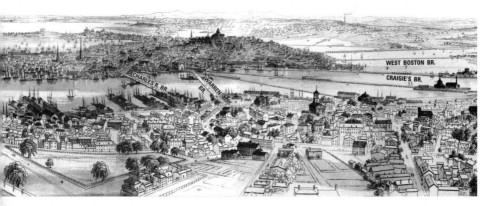

1848 view south from the Bunker Hill Monument

Museum of Science on the site of Craigie's Bridge, the Longfellow Bridge on the site of the West Boston Bridge, and the new Leonard P. Zakim Bunker Hill Bridge, which dominates the view.

Finally, compare the view of the Navy Yard from the last window with the *1848 view east from the Bunker Hill Monument* (line up the red brick Building 5 in both views). You can see Dry Dock 1 in both views and get a sense of the amount of land made by filling in timber docks—the enclosure on the waterfront in the *1848 view*. The latter view also shows the ropewalk and timber

1848 view east from the Bunker Hill Monument

shed visited on Walk 11 (♦ p. 180), though they are obscured from the present view by the elevated approach to the Tobin Bridge and by other buildings. The huge structures at the north end of the yard in the *1848 view east* are shiphouses in which ships as large as the *Constitution* were built.

5   **Descend the Bunker Hill Monument, cross Monument Square, go down Monument Street (opposite from the side you came up) to Bunker Hill Street at the bottom, cross Bunker Hill Street, turn right to the T bus stop, and catch a #93 bus to St. Francis de Sales Church (the large church on the right at the top of the hill). Cross Bunker Hill Street and go down Mead Street to the top of the stairs.**
From this point you can see how steep the south side of Bunker Hill is.

6   **Return to Bunker Hill Street, turn left, and go to Doherty Playground (Charlestown Heights).**

PUBLIC PARKS
Boston established a public park system in 1876. Although the park commissioners tried to locate a park in each section of the city, they did not include one in Charlestown on the grounds that there was no suitable space. But after years of petitions from Charlestown residents, in 1891 the commissioners purchased two sites for parks in Charlestown, one of which was the present Doherty Playground, which may still have been available because, as you'll see, it is very precipitous. The park, originally called Charlestown Heights and renamed Doherty Playground in 1942, was laid out by Frederick Law Olmsted, the designer of all the original Boston parks, and remains today much as he planned.

7   **Go through Doherty Playground.**
As you go through Doherty Playground (Charlestown Heights), note that the section near Bunker Hill Street is a shaded promenade, just as Olmsted planned. Beyond it, the original lawn now has a swimming pool, basketball courts, and a tot lot.

8   **Stop at the top of the terrace overlooking the Mystic River.**
From the terrace at the far end of the park you can get a good sense of the height of the north side of Bunker Hill. Here Olmstead's original routes down the hill—steps and a path lined with boulders of Roxbury puddingstone, a local conglomerate—are quite intact.
No landmaking was originally planned at Charlestown Heights. In 1895, however, a company dredging the Mystic River asked permission to dump the dredgings on the flats in front of the park. The park commissioners agreed and by 1898 a triangular area had been filled and covered with sand, creating what came to be called Dewey Beach (*see 1896 and 1907 charts*). In 1957 the parks department sold the beach, presumably because the Mystic had become too polluted for swimming, to the American Sugar Refinery Company, which then

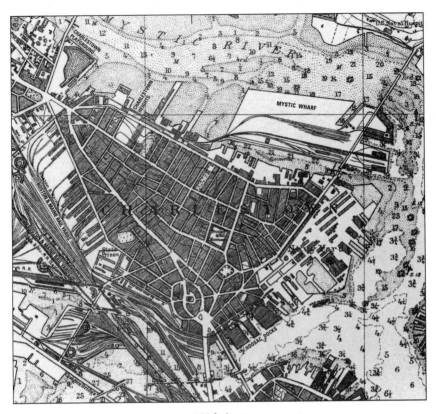

1896 chart

filled the rest of the flats and erected the building below (best seen when the leaves are off the trees). Actually, all the land north of Medford Street has been created by filling, as you can see on the *current street map*.

Go right and go down either the stairs or path to Medford Street, turn 9
left, and stop at the end of Medford Street at Bunker Hill Street.

MIDDLESEX CANAL

To your right, Main Street used to continue in a straight line and crossed the Middlesex Canal about where the rotary is now (*see current street map and 1818 and 1848 maps* in Walk 11, pp. 166 and 167). The Middlesex Canal was constructed between 1794 and 1803 as one of the first canals in the country and ran from the Charlestown mill pond (*see 1818 and 1848 maps and 1993 drawing* in Walk 11, pp. 166, 167, and 164—in the last, the canal is shown at the left-hand margin) to the Merrimack River near what is now Lowell, Massachusetts. The canal provided a convenient way to transport goods between Boston Harbor, which was connected to the Middlesex Canal via a canal through the former Mill Pond (see Walk 2, ♦ p. 40), and the Merrimack area. The Middlesex Canal flourished until it was superseded in the 1830s by

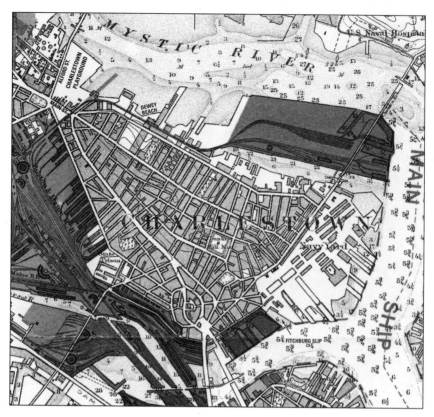

1907 chart

the Boston & Lowell Railroad, which ran on almost exactly the same route and could operate year-round while the canal was, of course, closed by ice in winter. After the canal ceased operating in 1853, the Charlestown section was filled in.

10 **Bear right onto Main Street, go past the fire station and Schrafft's building on your right, take the walk next to the chain-link fence on the west side of the Schrafft's building, and enter Ryan Playground through an iron gate between the tot lot and the Schrafft's building.**

PUBLIC PARKS (RESUMED)

The second area purchased in 1891 for a Charlestown park was this one, which at the time was a mill pond (*see 1879 map* in Walk 11, p. 168). The city began filling what was named Charlestown Playground in 1891 with rubbish, coal ashes, and dirt from other sites. By 1896 the northwest side of the mill pond had been filled (*see 1896 chart*), but the entire park wasn't completed until 1905 (*see 1907 chart*). Olmsted had originally planned gymnasiums, a promenade, and bath houses for the park, but, because Dewey Beach had been created in the interim (see p. 188), only one gymnasium and a running track were constructed. The park, which was renamed Ryan Playground in 1942, was originally used for ball games in the summer and skating in the winter; today it is devoted solely to baseball diamonds.

Go straight out along the side of Ryan Playground to HarborWalk on the river. 11
From this vantage point you can see all of Ryan Playground, all of which is made land, as well as wonderful views of the Mystic River.

This is the end of the walk. Nearest T station—Sullivan Square (Orange Line).

If you took this walk as a continuation of Walk 11, an alternate, and highly recommended, end to the walk is to take the water shuttle from the Navy Yard to Long Wharf for a wonderful view of Boston's waterfront. Return to Main Street and catch the #93 bus back to the Navy Yard (ask the driver for the correct stop). After leaving the bus, go under the Tobin Bridge, cross Chelsea Street, enter the Navy Yard, go down 5th Street and then to the left of Dry Dock 2 to the water shuttle landing.

At Long Wharf, the nearest T subway station is Aquarium (Blue Line).

Further Reading about Boston

Landmaking

Seasholes, Nancy S. *Gaining Ground: A History of Landmaking in Boston.* Cambridge, Mass.: The MIT Press, 2003.

Maps

Krieger, Alex, and David Cobb with Amy Turner, eds. *Mapping Boston.* Cambridge, Mass.: The MIT Press, 1999.

Digitized Boston maps at the Harvard Map Collection— http://lib.harvard.edu/catalogs/hollis.html "Hollis Catalog," Search Type: Title, Search For: Harvard Map Collection Digital Maps

Digitized Boston maps at the Boston Public Library— http://www.bpl.org/research/nblmapcenter.htm

History

Allison, Robert J. *A Short History of Boston.* Beverly, Mass.: Commonwealth Editions, 2004.

O'Connor, Thomas H. *The Hub: Boston Past and Present.* Boston: Northeastern University Press, 2001.

Historical Sites

Wilson, Susan. *Boston Sites & Insights: An Essential Guide to Historic Landmarks In and Around Boston.* Revised edition. Boston: Beacon Press, 2003.

Architectural Guides

Southworth, Susan, and Michael Southworth. *AIA Guide to Boston.* Second edition. Guilford, Conn.: Globe Pequot Press, 1992.

Lyndon, Donlyn. *The City Observed: Boston. A Guide to the Architecture of the Hub.* New York: Vintage Books, 1982.

Landscape History

Zaitzevsky, Cynthia. *Frederick Law Olmsted and the Boston Park System.* Cambridge, Mass.: Belknap Press of Harvard University Press, 1982.

Haglund, Karl. *Inventing the Charles River.* Cambridge, Mass.: The MIT Press, 2003.

Historical Photographs

Bergen, Philip. *Old Boston in Early Photographs, 1850–1918: 174 Prints from the Collection of The Bostonian Society.* New York: Dover Publications, 1990.

Campbell, Robert, and Peter Vanderwarker. *Cityscapes of Boston: An American City through Time.* Boston: Houghton Mifflin, 1992.

Vanderwarker, Peter. *Boston Then and Now: 59 Boston Sites Photographed in the Past and Present.* New York: Dover Publications, 1982.

McNulty, Elizabeth. *Boston Then and Now.* San Diego: Thunder Bay Press, 1999.

Digitized Boston photographs at The Bostonian Society— http://www.bostonhistory.org/ "Search"

ILLUSTRATION CREDITS

BA—Boston Athenaeum
BPL/P—Courtesy of the Boston Public Library, Print Department
BPL/RB—Boston Public Library/Rare Books Department
BRA—Boston Redevelopment Authority
Brookline—Courtesy of the Public Library of Brookline
DCR—Courtesy of the Department of Conservation and Recreation Archives, Boston
HMC—With permission of the Harvard Map Collection, Harvard College Library
HNE/SPNEA—Courtesy of Historic New England/SPNEA
LA—Sidney N. Shurcliff, "Boston's Proposed Development on the Charles River,"
   Landscape Architecture 40, no. 1 (1949): 20
MHS—Courtesy of the Massachusetts Historical Society
NPS Boston—Boston National Historical Park
NPS Olmsted—Courtesy of the National Park Service, Frederick Law Olmsted
   National Historic Site
SL—Courtesy of the State Library of Massachusetts
TBS—Courtesy of The Bostonian Society/Old State House
All current photos—Nancy S. Seasholes; preface photo, Jessicca Hosman

WALK 1—1676 map (MHS), 1722 map (HMC), 1852 map (BA), 1867 photo fr. Milk
St. (TBS), 1796 map (SL), 1814 map (BRA), 1849 view (SL), 1867 photo down Oliver
St. (TBS), 1826 map (HMC), c.1850 photo (TBS), 1743 view (Courtesy of the
American Antiquarian Society), 1789 engraving (BPL/P), 1824 engraving (James
Henry Stark, *Antique Views of ye Town of Boston* [Boston: Photo-electrotype Engraving
Co., 1882]), 1823 plan (BPL/RB), 1827 view (BPL/P), 1868 plan (MHS)

WALK 2—1807 map (SL), 1814 map (BRA), 1811 drawings (BPL/P), 1852 map
(BA)

Walk 3—1800 map (HMC), 1803 map (BPL/RB), 1826 map (HMC), 1852 map
(BA), 1853 photo (The Harvard Medical Library in the Francis A. Countway Library
of Medicine), 1870 bird's-eye (BPL/RB), 1892 photo (City of Boston, Archives and
Records Management Division), 1892 plan (NPS Olmsted), 1931 plan (DCR), 1949
plan (*LA*), 1913 photo (HNE/SPNEA), 1910 photo (DCR)

WALK 4—1803 map (BPL/RB), 1807 map (HMC), 1814 map (BRA), 1852 map
(BA), 1866 bird's-eye (BPL/RB), diagram (Harl P. Aldrich and James R. Lambrechts,
"Back Bay Boston, Part II: Groundwater Levels," *Civil Engineering Practice* 1, no. 2
[1986]: 35), 1870 photo (Courtesy of George Fanning), 1826 map (HMC), 1925 aerial (BPL/P), 1934 aerial (DCR)

WALK 5—1803 map (BPL/RB), 1826 map (HMC), 1835 map (HMC), 1868 photo (BPL/P), 1927 photo (HNE/SPNEA), 1861 map (TBS), 1871 map (TBS), 1839 engraving (TBS)

WALK 6—1821 map (John G. Hales, *Survey of Boston and Its Vicinity* . . .[Boston: Ezra Lincoln, 1821]), 1852 map (BA), 1850 bird's-eye (BPL/RB), 1858 photo (BPL/P), 1858 engraving (*Ballou's Pictorial Drawing-Room Companion* 15 [October 1858]: 209), c. 1859 photo (TBS), 1859 engraving (BPL/RB), c.1866 photo (TBS), 1869 photo (BPL/P), 1870 bird's-eye (BPL/RB), 1880s photo (BPL/P), 1863–1869 photo (BA), 1894 photos (DCR), 1908 photo (DCR), 1910 photo (DCR), 1919 photo (DCR), 1935 photo (DCR), 1934 photo (DCR), 1934 aerial (TBS), 1983 aerial (Alex S. MacLean/Landslides)

WALK 7—1836 map (TBS), 1879 plan (NPS Olmsted), c.1966 aerial (DCR), 1882 map (TBS), 1884 photo (BPL/P), 1888 map (TBS)

WALK 8—1891 photo (Brookline), 1892 photo of Muddy R. (NPS Olmsted), 1892 photo of Christ's Church (NPS Olmsted), 1900 photo (Brookline), 1882 map (TBS), 1888 map (TBS), 1931 plan (DCR), 1949 plan (*LA*), 1951 photo (DCR), c. 1954 photo (DCR)

WALK 9—1797 map (HMC), 1805 map (SL), 1832 map (HMC), 1835 map (HMC), 1838 map (BPL/RB), 1852 map (BA), 1896 chart (HMC), 1901 chart (HMC)

WALK 10—1775 view (HMC), 1814 map (BPL/RB), 1826 map (HMC), 1835 map (HMC), 1866 map (HMC), 1866 bird's-eye (BPL/RB), 1870 bird's-eye (BPL/RB), 1845 map (SL), 1852 map (HMC), c.1865 photo (TBS), 1950s aerial (TBS), 1896 chart (HMC), 1911 chart (HMC), 1934 chart (HMC), 1969 photo (BPL/P)

WALK 11—1993 drawing (Courtesy of Thomas Dahill, the artist), 1775 map (HMC), 1818 map (TBS), 1848 map (HMC), 1879 map (HMC), 1823 map (NPS Boston), 1834 map (NPS Boston), 1901 map (National Archives and Records Administration), 1950 map (NPS Boston)

WALK 12—1848 views (Richard P. Mallory, *Panoramic View from Bunker Hill Monument*, engraved by James Smillie [Boston: Redding, 1848]), 1896 chart (HMC), 1907 chart (SL)

ACKNOWLEDGMENTS

I wish to thank The MIT Press for agreeing to publish a book not in their usual repertoire and for the wonderful team with whom it has been a pleasure to work on yet another book: Ellen Faran, Director; Michael Sims, Managing Editor; Yasuyo Iguchi, Design Manager; Margy Avery in the acquisitions department (preceded by Lisa Reeve and Jessica Baker); Mary Reilly, Digital Manuscript/Art Coordinator; and Theresa Lamoureux, Production Manager. I also appreciate the work of Jonathan Wyss and Kelly Sandefer of Topaz Maps, Inc., who drafted all the walking tour maps. Finally, I am very grateful to all those who tested these walks, particularly Larry Cohen and Susan Worst, who did every single walk. The "testers" also included Margy Avery and friends, Jessica Baker, Lisa Reeve, Erika Valenti, and my students in HIST E-1633, "Boston's Topographical History," at the Harvard University Extension School, especially Dennis R. McCarthy, whose idea it was to add walking tours to the course.

INDEX

Page numbers in *italics* refer to illustrations.

Somerset Street, *30*, 3
Somerville, Massachusetts, *vi, x*, 43, 164, 166, 169
Southack Street, 62
Southampton Street, *144*, 146, 158, 160, 161
South Battery, 12
South Bay, *vi, x*, 134, 137, 141, 146, 147, 153, 154
enlarged, *144–145,* 146, 161
filled, 81, 146, 153–154, 157, 158, 159, 160
pollution in, 157–158, 159–160
wharves in, 153, 154, 157, 159, 160
South Bay Avenue, *144*, 158, 159, 160
South Bay Center, *145*, 146, 161
South Bay incinerator, 160, *160*
South Bay Lands project, 81, 151, 153–154, 156
South Boston, *vi, x*, 29, 133, 134, 136, 137, 139, 141, 146, 161
South Boston Bridge, 134, 135, 136, 140, 147, 151
South Boston Flats, 12
South Burying Ground, *144*, 155
South Cove, *vi, x*, 84, 133, 143, 146
wharf owners, 134, 136
South Cove Corporation, 141
filled South Cove, 136–138, 140, 146, 151, 161
Southeast Expressway, 85, 139, *145*, 157, 158, 160, *160*, 161
South End, 70–71*,* 72, *144*, 146
boundaries of, 80, 85

development of, 81, 100, 155
filled, 80, 81, 82
industries, 146, 148, 149, 150, 151, 154, 155
immigration and, 81, 152
squares, 72, 81
street grid, 80, 85
South Market building, *2*, 24
South Market Street, *2*, 23, 24
South Mill, 35
South Station, *132*, 133, 140, 141, 143, *143*
built, 85, 141, 142, 159
South Street, *132, 133,* 134, 136, 143
Southwest Corridor Park, 70, 72, 80, 84, 85, 86
Southwest Expressway, 85
SoWa District, 149, 150
Spaulding Rehabilitation Hospital, *31*, 42, 43
Stamp Act riots, 10
Staniford Street, *30, 44, 45*, 46
State House, *30*, 32, 37, 38, *39, 46, 58*, 59, 187
State Prison (Charlestown), 165–166, 186
State Street, *2*, 3, 8, 9, *9*, 14, 18, 19, 20, 21, 29
no. 60, *2*, 23
no. 75, 10
no. 114 (Richards Building), *2*, 21, 26
no. 150, *2*, 20–21, *20*
State Street Block, *2*, 19–20, *19*, 25
St. Botolph District, *70*, 72, 86
St. Botolph Street, *70*, 86
steam shovel, 92
Stedman's Cove, 114
St. Francis de Sales Church, 188
St. George Street, *144*, 154, 155

St. Germain Street, *70,* 87, *87*
Stillman Street, *31*, 34
St. James Avenue, *71*, 73, *88*, 99
no. 10, *88*, 99
St. James Hotel, 155
St. James the Greater Church, *132*, 136
St. Mary's Street, *120*, 125
Stoneholm Street, *108*, 113
Stony Brook, *vi, x*, 110, 111, 115, 116, 117, 118, 119, 122, 123
Stony Brook conduit, 115, 116
Stony Brook gatehouses, *108*, 116, *116*
Storrow, James J., Mrs., 67
Storrow Lagoon, *88*, 105, 107
Storrow Memorial, 107
Storrow Memorial Drive, *44, 45, 45*, 53, 54, 56, 57, 67, 68, 102, 107, 109, *120–121*, 128, 130, 131
tunnel, 55, 68
Storrow Memorial Embankment, 68
St. Stephen Street, *108*, 115
Stuart Street, *71*, 73, 98
Sudbury Street, *31*, 35, 36
Suffolk County Courthouse, old. *See* Adams, John, Courthouse
Suffolk County House of Correction, *144*, 158, 160
Suffolk Street, 77, 155
Suffolk Street District
filled, 76–77, 81
raised, 77, 82, 156–157
Sullivan Square, 40, 170, 186
Summer Street, *132*, 142, 143
Sumner Tunnel, 25
"Sunflower House," 65
Supreme Court, U.S., 171